Christ
and His
Seven Churches

What the Messages to the Seven Churches of Revelation Mean to Us Today

by

Carl A. DeLatte

Christ and His Seven Churches

All Scripture references are from the Authorized King James Version of the Bible, unless otherwise marked. References marked AMP are from the Amplified Bible, © Copyright 1987 by the Zondervan Corporation and the Lockman Foundation, La Habra, California.

All proceeds from the sale of this book will go to Healing Ministries, Inc., a nonprofit organization dedicated to publishing the Word of God through video Bible schools, the distribution of Bibles and Gospel tracts and other Christian literature.

Fairmont Books is a ministry of The McDougal Foundation, Inc., a Maryland nonprofit corporation dedicated to spreading the Gospel of the Lord Jesus Christ to as many people as possible in the shortest time possible.

Published by:

Fairmont Books
P.O. Box 3595
Hagerstown, MD 21742-3595
www.mcdougal.org

ISBN 1-884369-96-0

DEDICATION

I dedicate this book to two of the most pure-hearted people that I have ever had the privilege of serving God with:

To **PASTOR ROY STOCKSTILL**, with whom I was blessed to work as his associate for many years,

To my precious wife, **BETH DeLATTE**, to whom I have been married for more than thirty years.

Only God knows how much these two people have influenced my life and inspired me in His work.

ACKNOWLEDGMENTS

I would like to thank:

SISTER MAE PIERCE for her dedication in assisting me in proof-reading much of my manuscript

BROTHERS THAD PARRACK and CHARLES IMBODEN for helping with my computer when needed

Our daughter, JAWONNA GUILBEAU, for helping when needed in many aspects during the writing of this book

The many FELLOW LABORS who have supported our ministry

The many FELLOW PASTORS and CHRISTIAN FRIENDS who encouraged me to write

CONTENTS

FOREWORD BY ROY STOCKSTILL

Brother Carl DeLatte and I served on the same church staff for many years. He always blessed our congregation with strong Bible-based preaching, backed by the integrity of his Christian life. His discussion of the message to the Seven Churches of Revelation will challenge your heart to *"make your calling and election sure,"* and to be counted among the overcomers.

I am planning to join Brother Carl at the marriage Supper, and I hope you will join us there too.

Roy Stockstill
Pastor Emeritus
Bethany World Prayer Center

INTRODUCTION

During the early months of 1991, I died one night in my sleep. My spirit had already left my body, but it lingered above the bed in my room. I kept thinking that at any moment I would see Jesus, that He would come to take me. Several minutes seemed to pass as I was thinking, *Where is my Lord?* Then suddenly a message came to me from Heaven. It was just one word: "INCOMPLETE!"

What was incomplete? Apparently it was not yet my time to enter into Heaven, for my work on Earth was not complete. But it was more than my work that was not complete. I sensed that what God was doing in me personally was also not complete.

When this thought seized me, I said, "Lord, I have been preaching Your Word for the past thirty-nine years." But that did not seem to matter at the moment. I would not be received into the presence of God until I had finished my course here. Standing in the awesome presence of our Creator would require that the work begun in me by the Spirit be finished.

Paul's words written to the Philippians came to me:

Being confident of this very thing, that he which hath begun a good work in you will perform it until the day of Jesus Christ.
Philippians 1:6

To say the least, the Lord got my undivided attention that night, as I realized that there was much more for me yet to do here.

Since that fateful night in 1991, I have never once had to read the Bible to get a sermon for my next speaking engagement. Don't misunderstand me. I have read the Word more than ever before, but I have read it in a totally new way. It has become God's personal letter, written just for me. Every word has taken on a new meaning, and God has used the Word to wash me over and over again. Jesus said:

> *Now ye are clean through the word which I have spoken unto you.* John 15:3

Through His Word, God has been performing in me a cleansing of the heart and mind, of my actions and of my motives, so that the next time I leave this earthly tabernacle, I expect to see Him waiting for me and to hear Him say:

> *Well done, good and faithful servant; thou hast been faithful over a few things, I will make thee ruler over many things: enter thou into the joy of thy lord.* Matthew 25:23

I have learned more about Jesus and His Word in the past few years than I had learned in the previous thirty-nine years. The Lord spoke to me and told me He had brought me to this place so that I could publish His Word through video tapes, through ministers' Bible training schools, and through writing.

That's how this book came into being. May it be a blessing to your heart.

Carl A. DeLatte
Del Rio, Texas

CHAPTER 1

SEVEN LETTERS FROM JESUS

The Lord Jesus Christ sent a letter addressed to the angel of each of the seven churches of Asia minor. These letters represent the last recorded quotations from our Lord and the only words He ever spoke directly to the Church on Earth. In these letters, He foretold terrible calamities that would befall men, but He showed His concern for His Church by warning us before these things actually come to pass. He told the children of Israel:

> *The secret things belong unto the LORD our God: but those things which are revealed belong unto us and to our children for ever, that we may do all the words of this law.* Deuteronomy 29:29

While He was on the Earth, Jesus told His disciples:

> *Henceforth I call you not servants; for the servant knoweth not what his lord doeth: but I have called you friends; for all things that I have heard of my Father I have made known unto you.*
> John 15:15

> *Howbeit when he, the Spirit of truth, is come, he will guide you into all truth: for he shall not speak of himself; but whatsoever he shall hear, that shall he speak: and he will shew you things to come.* John 16:13

The Apostle Paul wrote to the Thessalonians:

Ye are all the children of light, and the children of the day: we are not of the night, nor of darkness.　　　1 Thessalonians 5:5

The Lord Jesus shows His Church the coming judgments and exhorts us to be overcomers. Sinners cannot be considered to be *"the children of the day"* nor *"the children of light,"* and until they are, Christ has only one message for them. It is a message of repentance from sin and of believing on the Lord Jesus Christ — while there is still time to do it.

Why Just These Seven Churches?

The seven churches to which these letters were written were not the only, nor the best-known, nor the largest churches of their day. The churches at Rome and Antioch were larger and more prominent, as were others. Why, then, were these specific churches chosen to receive these special letters?

These questions can only be answered by a close study of God's Word and through the guidance of the Holy Spirit. We don't know everything that God knows, but the Holy Spirit does. We are not infallible, but God is. After many hours of seeking God, searching the Scriptures, studying church history and reading what others have written on the subject, I believe that I have heard from God on this matter, and I will be sharing with you my conclusions as we progress.

Before we go any further, however, let us settle a very important point. What do we mean when we refer to "the Church"?

Who or What Is the Church Anyway?

The Greek word translated in our Bibles as "church" is *Ekklesia*.

It means "the called out ones." Called out of what? Called out of the world. The people who make up the Church of the Lord Jesus Christ are those who have not turned a deaf ear to Him.

The Apostle Paul, for instance, was called by God one day as he was traveling to Damascus. He later wrote of it:

Whereupon, O king Agrippa, I was not disobedient unto the heavenly vision.   Acts 26:19

Paul in his ignorance had been persecuting the Church when Jesus suddenly appeared to him. Paul gave his heart to Jesus that day and was born-again.

Those who have believed on the Lord Jesus Christ, have been washed in His blood and have been born again by His Spirit are part of His Church. We are those to whom God has revealed Himself in the person of the Lord Jesus Christ.

When Jesus asked His disciples, *"whom do men say that I the Son of man am?"* (Matthew 16:13), Peter answered, *"Thou art the Christ the Son of the living God"* (verse 16). It is very interesting to see what Jesus then said to Peter:

And Jesus answered and said unto him, Blessed art thou, Simon Barjona: for flesh and blood hath not revealed it unto thee, but my Father which is in heaven.   Matthew 16:17

On another occasion, Jesus taught:

No man can come to me, except the Father which hath sent me draw him: and I will raise him up at the last day.   John 6:44

God the Father draws us to the Savior by the Holy Spirit. It is not something we can do for ourselves. Paul wrote to the Corinthians:

... no man can say that Jesus is the Lord, but by the Holy Ghost.
1 Corinthians 12:3

We can't even say it without His help. This is God's work. It is His Church and He makes it from the "called out ones." Of them He forms a great Body that transcends all geographical, national and denominational barriers. Regardless of where one lives, regardless of the color of one's skin, regardless of the time in which one lived and regardless of the local church where one chooses to worship, there is only one Church.

Of this great throng, John wrote:

After this I beheld, and, lo, a great multitude, which no man could number, of all nations, and kindreds, and people, and tongues, stood before the throne, and before the Lamb, clothed with white robes, and palms in their hands; And cried with a loud voice, saying, Salvation to our God which sitteth upon the throne, and unto the Lamb. And all the angels stood round about the throne, and about the elders and the four beasts, and fell before the throne on their faces, and worshipped God, Saying, Amen: Blessing, and glory, and wisdom, and thanksgiving, and honour, and power, and might, be unto our God for ever and ever. Amen.
And one of the elders answered, saying unto me, What are these which are arrayed in white robes? and whence came they?
And I said unto him, Sir, thou knowest.
And he said to me, These are they which came out of great tribulation, and have washed their robes, and made them white in the blood of the Lamb. Revelation 7:9-14

In the Body of Christ, there are no language barriers, no limitations of any kind. In what has become a favorite Bible passage for millions of believers throughout the Earth, Jesus said:

For God so loved the world, that he gave his only begotten Son, that whosoever believeth in him should not perish, but have everlasting life. John 3:16

Although denominational divisions are a reality in the organized church, Jesus said:

Verily, verily, I say unto you, He that heareth my word, and believeth on him that sent me, hath everlasting life, and shall not come into condemnation; but is passed from death unto life. John 5:24

Anyone, therefore, who hears God's Word **and** believes on the Father (or commits himself to God), that **person** will be saved, regardless of church affiliation.

A friend of mine who lives in another country discovered part of a page from the Gospel of John among some ashes. There he read in his own language those immortal and powerful words: *"For God so loved the world that he gave his only begotten Son, that whosoever believeth in him should not perish but have everlasting life."* His heart was open, and he called out to God. His prayer was **very** simple:

God,

I don't know Your Son, but I believe You sent Him, and I want to know Him.

According to his testimony, it was as though his spirit caught on fire at that moment, and his life was instantly and permanently changed. He knew nothing about denominations, but God made him part of the Church anyway.

The night God saved me, I knew nothing about the differences between one denomination and another. Pastor J.W. Taylor told me that Jesus would come into my heart if I would repent and ask Him to save me. I sensed that the word I was hearing was not from Pastor Taylor but from Jesus Himself, and I rejoiced to hear it. I accepted that call and have been following the Lord now for the past forty-seven years.

The Church is not made up of denominations. It is made up of those who made a conscious decision to follow Jesus. He said:

> *And when he putteth forth his own sheep, he goeth before them, and the sheep follow him: for they know his voice. And a stranger will they not follow, but will flee from him: for they know not the voice of strangers.*   John 10:4-5

Here are three important things that Jesus taught His disciples concerning those who make up the Church:

1. His sheep hear His voice.

> *Verily, verily, I say unto you, He that heareth my word, and believeth on him that sent me, hath everlasting life, and shall not come into condemnation; but is passed from death unto life.*   John 5:24

When a person becomes disturbed about the wrongdoings in his or her life, that is the voice of God's Spirit convicting them of sin. Jesus said:

> *Nevertheless I tell you the truth; It is expedient for you that I go away: for if I go not away, the Comforter [Holy Spirit] will not come unto you; but if I depart, I will send him unto you. And*

*when he is come, he will reprove the world of sin, and of right-
eousness, and of judgment.* John 16:7-8

The Holy Spirit must convict us of sin and judgment before we
can ever give our hearts to Jesus. The next verses tells us why:

*Of sin, because they believe not on me; Of righteousness, because
I go to my Father, and ye see me no more; Of judgment, because
the prince of this world is judged.* John 16:9-11

One must first be convicted of sin and judgment or he will see
no need for a Savior. It is the convicting power of the Holy Spirit
that causes us to seek for a solution to the sin and the problem of
pending judgment. God shows us what is right and what is wrong
and reveals to us just how wrong our own heart is. If we refuse to
hear, refuse to let that convicting power bother us, then we have
rejected the Spirit's call to salvation.

2. His sheep know His voice.

For they know his voice. John 10:4

Jesus Christ is our shepherd, and we know His voice. Jesus told
Pilate:

Everyone that is of the truth heareth my voice. John 18:37

We do not only know His voice, but we love His voice. Every
child of God should expect to hear God's voice daily, and some of
us are not satisfied unless we hear His voice many times a day.
The very worst thing that could ever happen to us would be not
to be able to hear His voice. The psalmist concurred. He said:

How sweet are thy words unto my taste! yea, sweeter than honey to my mouth!   Psalm 119:103

3. His sheep follow Him.

And a stranger will they not follow, but will flee from him: for they know not the voice of strangers.   John 10:5

Jesus is the only shepherd for us. We refuse to follow a stranger, and Satan is certainly a stranger to us. John said,

(But) he who commits sin (who practices evildoing) is of the devil,"
1 John 3:8, AMP

Some people claim to be followers of Jesus, but they also live a life of sin. Some claim to be Christians, and yet they follow any crowd that comes along. The message of the Lord for those people is the same message the apostle Peter gave in his day:

Wherefore the rather, brethren, give diligence to make your calling and election sure.   2 Peter 1:10

Being a part of Christ's Church is not based upon which part of the planet Earth you happen to live on, and it is not based upon which congregation you choose to worship and fellowship with. While it is helpful to the longevity of our faith to stay in a Bible-believing church where the people really love God and each other, this is not a qualification for salvation.

Have you heard His voice (His call to salvation)? Do you know His voice? Do you follow Him (obeying His Word to love God with all your heart and your neighbor as yourself)? If so, you can be assured that you belong to Jesus. I congratulate you and encourage you to keep this faith to the end.

GROWING IN FAITH

To help you to grow in the faith, I encourage you to be in a Bible-believing church. Fellowship with people of a common experience. Gather together and join in worshiping the Lord, in studying His Word. Speak of your Lord openly and often. Never be ashamed of Him.

Sports fans, when they get together, talk about their favorite ball teams, especially if their team happens to be winning at the moment. Well, Jesus won the greatest contest ever. He defeated our greatest adversary, Satan. We are proud of our Winner, and when we get together, He is always there in the midst of us. We make up His jewels:

> *Then they that feared the* LORD *spake often one to another: and the* LORD *hearkened, and heard it, and a book of remembrance was written before him for them that feared the* LORD, *and that thought upon his name. And they shall be mine, saith the* LORD *of hosts, in that day when I make up my jewels; and I will spare them, as a man spareth his own son that serveth him.*
>
> Malachi 3:16-17

When I came to know the Lord it was not because of any good thing I had done myself. I was living in sin, but Jesus loved me nevertheless. The Holy Spirit convicted me of sin and judgment, and I knew it was His voice that was calling me to repent and give Him control of my heart. I knew that my life was one big mess, and Jesus was showing me that He wanted to take charge and be my Lord. His purpose was to give me a more abundant life. Ever since the day I repented and asked Jesus to save me and to come into my heart, I have been in a church fellowship. But that was not what saved me. Christ made me part of His glorious Church.

THE PURPOSE OF THE LETTERS

I see three purposes for the letters Christ wrote to His churches:

1. They were to be read in all the churches. It was a custom among the early believers to read the letters written by the apostles in each and every church. Although a letter may have been written for a certain church, everyone could learn from its contents. As God was writing to one church, He was actually addressing all believers of all ages. He was saying then, as He says now:

   He that hath an ear, let him hear what the Spirit saith unto the churches.   Revelation 3:22

   We must give God a chance to speak to us personally by paying close attention to the message given to each church and applying those words to our own individual situations. Everything that Jesus said to the churches has been helpful to me. The exhortation that He gave to the church at Smyrna, for example, was especially helpful to me during the time I pastored my first church. My salary was only twenty-five dollars a week. When I read what Jesus said to that church, I was encouraged. He said:

   I know your poverty, but you are rich.

   On other occasions, when people would leave the church I was pastoring for no apparent reason, I would be encouraged by Jesus' word to the church at Sardis:

   Strengthen the things which remain.

2. The seven churches of Revelation represent, in the order they are presented, the characteristics of the Church as a whole in a certain period of church history. For instance, Ephesus, the first church mentioned to John, represented the earliest church period, from 33 to 100 A.D. The second church mentioned was Smyrna, and Smyrna represented the second era of church history, from 100 to 313 A.D. The other churches, in the same way, represented other periods and the message was for God's people in those periods. Still, each of the letters can speak to us and can meet our own spiritual needs.

3. God had a message for each of the seven churches in Asia Minor, He had a message for each of the other churches that existed during John's time, He had a message for the church of every generation of time, and He has a message for each church in existence today. This is proven by the prophetic relationship with which Jesus identified Himself to each particular church and by its application to each individual church, and each church period.

Jesus' Identity and Message to the Churches Call for Attention and Action

To each of the seven churches, Jesus identified Himself in a different way, and the way He identified Himself was important to the message He was about to deliver. If you received a letter marked as coming to you from the IRS, you would know immediately that the message inside that letter demanded serious attention. Personally, I believe that every message written in the Bible deserves serious attention on our part, especially these messages that came directly from Jesus to His Church on Earth.

I take these letters very seriously and very personally, and my faith and commitment to Jesus Christ has been strengthened by studying them. I have also been blessed by studying church history, the history of the location of each of the local churches mentioned and by all the rest of the research required to write this book. I was blessed, most of all, because much prayer was involved in the preparation of this book. As the message of our Lord to the churches penetrated deeply into my own heart, I spent time in conviction and repentance of my shortcomings as a believer and in growing and maturing spiritually. This is important to each of us.

In writing this book, I wanted to hear from God, just as the disciples had been instructed to do in their day on the Mount of Transfiguration:

And there was a cloud that overshadowed them: and a voice came out of the cloud, saying, This is my beloved Son: hear him.
Mark 9:7

It is my prayer that His messages of these seven letters will do as much for you as they have for me.

There are some interesting and meaningful patterns to be found in these seven letters. Each letter, for instance, carries a commendation. The other common elements we will look at include a rebuke, an exhortation, a warning and a promise. We will also look at each of the cities and their unique characteristics and circumstances. We will conclude each study with an analysis of the relationship between the way the Lord identified Himself to the church with the message He gave.

THE BATTLE AGAINST SATAN

One of the first things we notice about the various churches was that they all had their struggles. They all faced a common enemy. People in every generation and in every physical location have been affected spiritually by the culture of their day. Satan has set himself up as the little god of this world. As Paul wrote:

In whom the god of this world hath blinded the minds of them which believe not. 2 Corinthians 4:4

When Adam disobeyed God, he fell from his original state. Taking advantage of Adam's weakness, Satan stole from him the dominion he had received from the Creator and set himself up as god in this world. Since that time men are drawn to the things of this world by nature rather than to the things of God. While it is not wrong to possess things (we need them to exist), God's desire is that we delight in our relationship with Him more than in the things around us. Satan, however, with his control of the culture of the time, exerts a massive influence over the hearts of men, drawing them away from God and into his web of deceit.

Satan uses every possible tool to keep us from God, and he makes sure that society around us pulls us downward, rather than Heavenward. We will, therefore, examine the cultural conditions under which each of these churches existed so that we can see what they had to overcome. An examination of our own culture is also in order so that we can overcome the evil traps of our own times.

As we move forward now, I hope you will find it as exciting as I do to investigate the letters of Jesus to His churches.

CHAPTER 2

CHRIST'S LETTER
TO THE CHURCH IN EPHESUS

Unto the angel of the church of Ephesus write; These things saith he that holdeth the seven stars in his right hand, who walketh in the midst of the seven golden candlesticks; I know thy works, and thy labour, and thy patience, and how thou canst not bear them which are evil: and thou hast tried them which say they are apostles, and are not, and hast found them liars: And hast borne, and hast patience, and for my name's sake. Revelation 2:1-3

In this very first verse Jesus identifies Himself to the church in Ephesus. As we go along, we will see how that identity relates to the message of the letter, as we deal with each of the seven churches in order. The Church in Ephesus corresponds to the earliest period of Church history, the first century.

THE CITY

Ephesus was a large city with an excellent harbor. It had one of the best marketplaces in Asia. It was, however, a city of immorality, paganism, heathenism, materialism and the home of the false teachers of Nicolaitanism.

The Temple of Diana was located in Ephesus and the activities surrounding the temple brought in a very large revenue for the citizens of the town (see Acts 19:23-25). People came to Ephesus from many heathen nations to worship the "great" goddess Diana. They came to visit her "sacred" museum which held masterpieces of sculpture and paintings.

God delights, however, in working in the midst of darkness. In Ephesus, He showed His mighty hand through the apostle Paul:

And God wrought special miracles by the hands of Paul: So that from his body were brought unto the sick handkerchiefs or aprons, and the diseases departed from them, and the evil spirits went out of them.   Acts 19:11-12

The teaching of Paul in the city counteracted the false teaching of the Nicolaitans. They taught that it did not matter what one did in the flesh. The flesh is corrupt and could not be controlled. Paul refuted that:

I beseech you therefore, brethren, by the mercies of God, that ye present your bodies a living sacrifice, holy, acceptable unto God, which is your reasonable service. And be not conformed to this world: but be ye transformed by the renewing of your mind, that ye may prove what is that good, and acceptable, and perfect, will of God.   Romans 12:1-2

The fact that God was doing this great and unusual miracle through Paul may have spoken to them more than his teaching. God was showing the Nicolaitans that God sanctified the body of Paul and made him a living sacrifice — holy and acceptable unto God.

A great revival broke out in Ephesus, and genuine signs of repentance and new life were visible:

And many that believed came, and confessed, and shewed their deeds. Many of them also which used curious arts brought their books together, and burned them before all men: and they counted the price of them, and found it fifty thousand pieces of silver. So mightily grew the word of God and prevailed. Acts 19:18-20

God is never limited by the presence of workings of Satan. God always has a way of outshining the deceiver wherever His Gospel is preached. The city of Ephesus witnessed the mighty works of God.

THE COMMENDATION

I know thy works, and thy labour, and thy patience, and how thou canst not bear them which are evil: and thou hast tried them which say they are apostles, and are not, and hast found them liars: And hast borne, and hast patience, and for my name's sake hast laboured, and hast not fainted.
But this thou hast, that thou hatest the deed of the Nicolaitans, which I also hate. Revelation 2:2-3 and 6

Let us examine the various parts of this commendation:

I know thy works: This church was very zealous to do good works and service for God. Twice the letter speaks of their labor for the name of Jesus. They loved to work for Jesus. They were hard-working people, ready to do whatever needed to be done for the Lord.

And thy patience: The Greek word translated "patience" here means "steadfastness, unswerving, loyal regardless of trials, sufferings, persecutions, etc." This is a qualification that we must all have if we expect to endure to the end. The Christians of this church were strong in the faith and this fact was shown by their good works.

Canst not bear them which are evil: The Ephesian believers took a strong stand against evil. They were uncompromising in their convictions. Their lives were clean, pure, honest and loyal. Therefore, they could not bear people who were evil: gossipers, enviers, strivers, false teachers, etc.

Thou hast tried them which say they are apostles, and are not, and hast found them to be liars: The Ephesian church had been taught well by Paul, John and other teachers. They rejected Christian counterfeits.

And hast borne: These men and women knew what it took to stand. In Paul's letter to them, he exhorted them to be strong in the Lord that they could stand against the wiles of the devil (see Ephesians 6:10-14). They heeded this message.

And hast not fainted: These Christians had not grown weary. Paul, in his letter to the church at Galatia, said, *"And let us not be weary in well doing: for in due season we shall reap, if we faint not"* (Galatians 6:9). This church was not made up of a bunch of weary pilgrims, despite the fact that they were in an intensive period of harvest.

But this thou hast, that thou hatest the deed of the Nicolaitans, which I also hate: The Nicolaitans taught that the body was defiled already, so it did not matter what one did in the flesh. It was only the spirit that mattered. The church at Ephesus is commended by the Lord for hating this teaching. God hates sin and false teaching and so should we. Regardless of how popular or how acceptable sin becomes in any society, it is still not acceptable to God.

THE REBUKE

Nevertheless I have somewhat against thee, because thou hast left thy first love.   Revelation 2:4

After hearing such wonderful commendations, one would think that the church in Ephesus might well be perfect, but it was not so. Jesus said that he had something against them. The people of this church worked hard for the Lord, were steadfast in their faith, had strong conviction against evil, knew the apostles' doctrine and rejected counterfeits and were not weary in their well doing, but, alas, they had left their "first love." What did Jesus say about love?

Thou shalt love the Lord thy God with all thy heart, and with all thy soul, and with all thy mind. This is the first and great commandment. And the second is like unto it, Thou shalt love thy neighbour as thyself. On these two commandments hang all the law and the prophets.   Matthew 22:37-40

Love is the main ingredient of the Christian faith. It is indispensable. Without love, Paul showed us, we are nothing:

Though I speak with the tongues of men and of angels, and have not charity, I am become as sounding brass, or a tinkling cymbal. And though I have the gift of prophecy, and understand all mysteries, and all knowledge; and though I have all faith, so that I could remove mountains, and have not charity, I am nothing.   1 Corinthians 13:1-2

Love is a choice. Before we can love, we must choose to keep God's commandment, to put it into practice. When we fail to do that, we have left the call to God's love.

The Lord had something against the church in Ephesus, and that is a terrible thing. If we cannot show His love to the world, after He has shown His love and forgiveness to us, no wonder He has something against us.

What could have happened to cause the Ephesian believers to lose their first love? It may have been any or all of the following:

1. The lost influence of the apostles

As the first century came to a close, all the apostles had been martyred except John, and he was an old man by this time. Ignatius, the first Christian historian, wrote that John was old and feeble. When asked to speak, he would always say, " Saints, love one another." When they asked him why he always said that same thing, he replied, "Because Jesus said for us to love one another, for love is of God." The apostles were eyewitnesses of Jesus, and they had a deep love for Him. Their hearts were bonded to Jesus and to one another. This love flowed down from the apostles to churches they established and ministered to.

2. The lost influence of other departed saints

As we have seen, the city of Ephesus witnessed many miracles. The older saints had witnessed the beginning of the church, the mighty revival and the powerful teaching of the apostles, but most of all they had seen the extraordinary love that the apostles had for Jesus and for others, and that love had flowed down to them. Now, by the time this letter was written, most of these older saints had departed and gone to be with the Lord. With their departure, the church had lost the strong influence they could exert on the younger converts.

Believe me, I am not saying this just because I an older believer, but our churches need to pay closer attention to the teaching of the apostle Paul about honoring our elders (see 1 Timothy 5:1 and 17). Pastor Roy Stockstill, who was my pastor for many years, has my deepest respect. His life and teaching made a major impact on my life. I will always give him and any other elder my uttermost respect. The Word of God teaches us to do it, and it is there for a reason.

3. A lack of influence on the part of the incumbent pastor

It is possible that the pastor who followed the apostle John was strong in the faith and a good teacher, organizer and planner, while, at the same time, lacking in his love for Jesus or for the flock. The Lord called the pastor of these churches "the star" that He held in His hand. They were, He said, the messengers of the church. A pastor is, by far, the greatest influence on any church. A congregation, generally speaking, will never rise above the spiritual level of its pastor. It is very possible that the incumbent pastor had all the good qualities that Jesus commended the church for, but was lacking in the fervent love that Paul and John possessed for Jesus Christ and for His sheep. Regardless of our talents, the love of God must flow through us and down to the church or we cannot please our heavenly Father and show His light to the world. If it is true that the pastor was lacking in this regard, it is not difficult to see how his lack could infect the entire church.

4. The influence of the world

Ephesus was infested with paganism, prostitution, materialism and many other forms of ungodliness. Satan always tries to use this world system to draw our affections away from God. God is love and wants us to be like him, but many feel drawn back to the world. It would not have been unusual if this was the case in Ephesus.

5. The temporary lull in the persecution of the church

The church age began with the outpouring of the Holy Spirit on the Day of Pentecost, and, although the early Christians were persecuted by their fellow Jews, their Roman rulers extended them freedom to worship as they chose. This lull in action was not necessarily good for the young church, which has always shown greater strength during times of difficulty. Trials and tribulations keep us close to the Lord and dependent on His goodness.

THE EXHORTATION

Remember therefore from whence thou art fallen.

Revelation 2:5

The church at Ephesus is a picture of the Apostolic age. The apostles had provided the primitive church with excellent leadership, and it was founded upon apostolic doctrine. The believers had broken ties with tradition in order to follow the teachings of Christ. They had served Him with love and joy, without complaint, for they were strong in the faith. They hated sin, and their doctrines were pure and true. As the first century drew to a close, however, their love for Jesus began to wane. More and more, they served Him out of a sense of duty rather than out of a heart of love. When they had served Him with a heart of love, they had also served Him with a fullness of joy. No task had been too hard, no sacrifice too great for the One they loved. Now that was changing.

The story has been told of two orphan boys. One very cold morning two homeless and hungry boys showed up at a boy's home. They knocked on the door, and a very godly man came to open the door. He saw that one of the boys was carrying the other one on his back because he was crippled. "Oh! Come in and put your friend down," he said. "He must be very heavy."

"No sir," the boy replied, "he's not heavy, he's my brother."

When we serve Jesus with a loving heart because He's our brother who died for us, His burden will always be light and His yoke will always be easy.

When Roy Stockstill was senior pastor in my home church, I was privileged to serve with him as one of his associates. Everything the man did he did for God. His relationship with his staff and with the members of the church was one of great love. He had a pure heart, and did everything with integrity. Needless to say, this spirit influenced his son Larry, the current pastor, and every believer in the church. The writer of Hebrews has declared:

And let us consider one another to provoke unto love and to good works: Hebrews 10:24

The church in Ephesus was encouraged by the Lord to remember the place they had fallen from. It is always sad when Christians have to remember more joyful days. If we would only grow in love and faith, instead of decreasing in these areas, it would never be necessary to look back to better times. God wants these to be the very best of times for all of us.

THE WARNING

Repent, and do the first works; or else I will come unto thee quickly, and will remove thy candlestick out of his place, except thou repent. Revelation 2:5

Let us examine the various elements of this warning:

Repent: Repentance demands action. If a person says that he has repented, but he continues in the same lifestyle, then his "repentance" is in vain. When Paul repented that day on the road to Damascus, he totally abandoned his former style of living. When I repented in 1952 I had to develop a whole new way of living. True repentance causes us to hate our former lifestyle and to abandon it.
Jesus preached repentance:

Repent ye, and believe the gospel.   Mark 1:15

Peter preached repentance on the Day of Pentecost:

Repent, and be baptized.   Acts 2:38

Paul preached repentance everywhere he went:

Testifying both to the Jews, and also to the Greeks, repentance toward God, and faith toward our Lord Jesus Christ.
Acts 20:21

Repent and turn to God.   Acts 26:20

If we are interested in God's promises, we must be willing to follow the commands He has attached to them. Jesus said:

If ye love me, keep my commandments.   John 14:15

Personally, I don't believe that our Lord's commandments are burdensome. The only heavy pull I have experienced in my life has been when I was not yoked to the Lord. I have been serving Him for nearly half a century now and have found Him to be "meek and lowly of heart." He is not a hard taskmaster, as many imagine.

And do the first work: The *"first works"* of the church in Ephesus were pleasing unto the Lord. These early disciples served God out of a heart of love, and that is the service He requires. This church praised, worshipped, took communion, witnessed, gave, prayed, helped the needy, studied God's Word and helped the pastor of the church, and they did it all with the love of God in their hearts. Now, Jesus wanted them to return to those "first works," return to the works that were the fruit of love.

Or else I will come quickly: Our Lord is longsuffering, full of mercy and slow to anger. He gives us all plenty of time in which to respond to His Word. When He comes, however, there will be no time for change. He will come *"quickly."* Six times in the book of Revelation, He said that He would come *"quickly."* In that unexpected moment, it will be too late for change, and those who are not ready must accept the consequences. Jesus went on to describe some of the consequences:

And will remove thy candlestick out of his place, except thou repent: The candlestick represents the Church. The Church gives light to the community and to the world. If Jesus were to remove the church from Ephesus, there would be nothing but spiritual darkness in that city. The Word of God would not be preached there, and eventually all the offspring in that place would walk in darkness. And that is exactly what happened in Ephesus. Present day Efes, the ruins of ancient Ephesus, lies in Muslim Turkey today. The people are forbidden by law to convert to any other faith.

THE PROMISE

He that hath an ear, let him hear what the Spirit saith unto the churches: To him that overcometh will I give to eat of the tree of life, which is in the midst of the paradise of God.

Revelation 2:7

Let us examine the various elements of this promise:

To him that overcometh will I give to eat of the tree of life, which is in the midst of the paradise of God: What a wonderful promise — full restoration! Everything that Adam lost and more will be returned to the overcomers. This time around, Satan will not be permitted to spoil things as he did for Adam. The "no trespassing" sign will be removed from the garden, and every overcomer will be invited in to eat the fruit from the tree of life in the midst of the garden.

Recently scientists have discovered that a deficiency in the human body is the cause of aging. I am sure that only the fruit of God's tree of life can restore that which is deficient. Scientists will never find the answer in their test tubes. Only the overcoming Christians will be permitted to eat the fruit from that tree.

He that hath an ear, let him hear what the Spirit saith unto the churches: God has given each of us ears, but not everyone wants to hear what He has to say. Here God is saying that if you have an ear that desires to hear, then listen to what the Spirit is saying to the churches. Every individual who has a heart hungry for God is invited to hear (understand) what the Spirit says to the churches. It is my prayer that your ears be not dull of hearing and that you have an open heart for God.

The Lord Jesus Christ spoke these same words to all seven of the churches of Revelation, showing that it is a message for all. The knowledge and understanding we gain of Christ and His Word is totally dependent upon how much we hunger to know. If we are satisfied to know only a few chosen doctrines, then God will serve us on a much smaller plate.

Some scriptures puzzled me for years, but I had a burning desire to understand them, and I would continue to pray, seek and knock, and suddenly one day the Spirit of God would *"light my candle."* As the psalmist declared:

For thou wilt light my candle: the LORD my God will enlighten my darkness.   Psalm 18:28

Many times the Lord has awakened me at odd hours of the night to reveal a scripture or scriptures to me because I hungered to know. God won't bother those who don't want to be bothered. To me, however, the sweet Word of God is better than sleep.

THE RELATIONSHIP BETWEEN THE IDENTITY AND THE MESSAGE

These things saith he that holdeth the seven stars in his right hand, who walketh in the midst of the seven golden candlesticks.
                                        Revelation 2:1

This is the way Jesus identified Himself to the church in Ephesus and to the first church era. Let us examine the various elements of this identity and see how they relate to the message He gave them:

He that holdeth the seven stars in his right hand: Jesus gave us the interpretation of the mystery of the seven stars. He said:

The seven stars are the angels of the seven churches.
Revelation 1:20

I tend to agree with the commentary of Rev. C.I. Scofield in his *New Scofield Study Bible.* This word angel, from the Greek word *aggelos*, is often translated "messenger" and represents anyone who bears God's messages to a church. Jesus is saying here that He holds the pastor (messenger) in His right hand. Just as he held Paul, Peter, John and the other apostles, He also holds each messenger of the Church in His right hand. The Word of God did not die with the apostles.

Jesus Christ the same yesterday, and to day, and for ever.
Hebrews 13:8

What God did through the apostles He would do through the messengers that replaced them. The Word of God, the power of the name of Jesus, the gifts of the Holy Spirit and the fullness of God's power were still available to the church at Ephesus and they are still available to us today. Everything that flows from the hand of Jesus would flow through His messengers to the church at Ephesus and it should be so in our churches today.

Who walketh in the midst of the seven golden candlesticks: Jesus gave us the interpretation of the mystery of the seven golden candlesticks as well:

The seven candlesticks which thou sawest are the seven churches.
Revelation 1:20

Jesus is saying that He walks in the midst of His churches. Where Jesus is, there is light, and His light must flow through the Church and into the community.

Jesus ministers to His Church through His messengers. He walks in the midst of His Church giving revelation (light). Then the Church must share this light with the world. It is God's light that will bring life, growth and healing to mankind. If Jesus were to remove the candlestick, then darkness would take the place of light, and we all know the tragic result of darkness.

CHAPTER 3

CHRIST'S LETTER
TO THE CHURCH IN SMYRNA

And unto the angel of the church in Smyrna write; These things
saith the first and the last, which was dead, and is alive.

Revelation 2:8

This is the way Jesus identified Himself to the church in Smyrna.
Later we will see how this identity relates to the message our Lord
gives to this church. The church in Smyrna represented the his-
toric period of the Church from about 100 to 313 A.D.

THE CITY

Smyrna, located some forty miles north of Ephesus, was a beautiful city known for its magnificent harbor. People commonly
referred to Smyrna as a flower, an ornament, and as the crown of
Asia. The Acropolis in Smyrna was circled with flowers, a hedge
and myrtle trees. The city dated to about two thousand years before Christ and during New Testament days had a thriving
economy, mainly because it was on the main trade route from
Rome to India and Persia. Many Jews lived in Smyrna, but the
population was predominantly pagan.

On the main street of Smyrna, known as "the street of gold," stood two temples dedicated to Zeus and another dedicated to Cybele, whom the locals considered to be "the mother of the gods." Smyrna was also the center of emperor worship during the time of the Roman Empire, and it contained a temple dedicated to Emperor Tiberius Caesar.

Smyrna, modern Izmir, is still in existence today and is located in Turkey. It is, as you might imagine, a tourist attraction for Christians who go there to see the sites of the early churches. Also to be seen in Smyrna are the ruins of the stadium where Polycarp, Bishop of Smyrna and disciple of the apostle John, was martyred. He was burned alive there in 155 A.D.

As Ephesus represented the apostolic church, so Smyrna represented the martyred church, covering a period from 100 to 313 A.D. With the passing of that era, the persecution of Christians in Smyrna and all over the Roman Empire came to an end.

THE COMMENDATION

I know thy works, and tribulation, and poverty, (but thou art rich) and I know the blasphemy of them which say they are Jews, and are not, but are the synagogue of Satan.   Revelation 2:9

Let us examine the various elements of this commendation:

I know thy works: Every good work that the church in Smyrna had done for the glory of God had been recorded and there were many. This is interesting in the light of the fact that thousands of Christians in Smyrna were martyred for their faith. Jesus knew each of them by name and their works would follow them.

And tribulation: The church in Smyrna experienced tribulation (a time of trouble) because of strong persecution. God has the right to allow every Christian's faith and works to be tested. Concerning the testing of our faith, Peter wrote:

That the trial of your faith, being much more precious than of gold that perisheth, though it be tried with fire, might be found unto praise and honour and glory at the appearing of Jesus Christ.

1 Peter 1:7

Paul wrote concerning this matter:

Every man's work shall be made manifest: for the day shall declare it, because it shall be revealed by fire; and the fire shall try every man's work of what sort it is. If any man's work abide which he hath built thereupon, he shall receive a reward.

1 Corinthians 3:13-14

The *"fire"* that *"revealed"* the works of this church was the suffering and physical death that many were called to face, but there has always been some type of *"fire"* at work revealing the faith of every Christian and determining its value. Sometimes the test of our faith reveals just the opposite of the test that the Smyrna church experienced. Sometimes our faith is found lacking. While some have passed the test of the *"fire"* of tribulation, others have excelled only in fame, riches, high position, power, prestige or the lust of the flesh.

Clarence Matheny, a good friend of mine, ministered behind the Iron Curtain during the Cold War period. He told the story of his conversation with an elderly Russian Christian lady. When he asked her if she would like to live in the United States, she replied, "No. I know that I can keep the faith here in Russia, even though we are strongly persecuted, but I'm not sure if I could stand the temptations of the riches of America." Many have failed that test.

And poverty: Poverty denotes the lack of material possessions. Most of the members of the church in Smyrna came from the poorer classes. Many who had been wealthy when they were converted to Christ were reduced to poverty because their property was confiscated. Others chose to give their wealth to the church to be used for the benefit of the whole Christian community. Jesus recognized the material lack the Smyrna believers suffered, yet still He said to them, *"but thou art rich."* These men and women had Jesus Christ in their hearts, and there are no greater riches. In all of God's creation there is nothing better to be found than Jesus. The church in Smyrna may have been poor in worldly goods and they may have faced tribulation, but they loved Jesus and they loved each other. Those who have Him have the very best, regardless of the status of their bank accounts. Personally, I would rather live in a grass hut and have Jesus than to live in the finest mansion, have all the riches of this world, and have to live without Him. We will see later what Jesus had to say to the church that thought it was rich.

I know the blasphemy of them that say they are Jews, and are not, but are the synagogue of Satan: This is not an anti-Jewish statement. God loves the Jewish people and will one day restore their kingdom. Jesus will sit on the throne of David and rule over the people of Zion (see Isaiah 9:6-7). We will talk about this later, but in order to understand this statement that Jesus made about the Jews, one must understand what Paul said:

For they are not all Israel, which are of Israel.   Romans 9:6

The people of Israel were raised up by God to form a righteous nation. The resulting nation, as we all know, has not always conformed to God's plan. But God's plan has not been defeated. Those who have not lived righteously have not qualified in His eyes as true Israelites. This same thing can be said of the Church. Christ died so that His Church might be holy and righteous. Since not everyone calling himself a Christian has been willing to live holy, we could say: "For they are not all Christians, who are of Christianity." People are not always what they claim to be. That was clearly the case with these who that called themselves Jews.

It seems very likely that these were among those who, we are told, made a good living by reporting against the Christians in Smyrna. If their "tip" led to the arrest of Christians, they were rewarded with ten percent of the possessions confiscated from those particular believers. Jesus refused to identify these men as Jews. They were, He said, *"the synagogue of Satan."*

THE REBUKE

There was no rebuke for the church in Smyrna, and this is notable. This church must have been *"without spot or wrinkle."* How could this be? Well this church suffered more persecution than any other in early church history. This persecution (*"the trial by fire"*) must have cleaned out all the hypocrites from the church. Those who were lustful, proud, arrogant, envious, striving, unforgiving, selfish and hateful simply could not stand the fire and got out. Those who were consumed by the love of money left. Those who were only interested in prestige were long gone.

Because the Christians never knew at what moment some Roman soldiers might show up at their house or place of business to arrest them and confiscate all that they had, this brought an unusual seriousness to their group. The choice for those who were arrested was denial of their faith or death, so that was serious business.

There was something very special about the faith of the believers in Smyrna. They were looking forward to seeing Jesus, either because of death or through His return, and they never knew what moment this might happen. This hope kept them pure. John wrote to the churches:

Beloved, now are we the sons of God, and it doth not yet appear what we shall be: but we know that, when he shall appear, we shall be like him; for we shall see him as he is. And every man that hath this hope in him purifieth himself, even as he is pure.

1 John 3:2-3

Too many Christians have dreaded the thought of death because they have so many possessions down here. They have it so nice they hate to leave this world behind. The day may well come when Christians will again be stripped of their worldly possessions. Let's not wait until that moment to get ready to live in God's presence. Moments like these, however, have their purpose. Perhaps it will only be in the moment of Church vs. the World that we truly become one in Christ. Will it take severe persecution to get us back into proper fellowship with God and with each other? Will it take severe persecution to get all the spots and wrinkles out of the Body of Christ and to strip us of all the garbage that has attached to us by our living in the world? Time will tell.

THE EXHORTATION

Fear none of those things which thou shalt suffer: behold, the devil shall cast some of you into prison, that ye may be tried; and ye shall have tribulation ten days: be thou faithful unto death.

Revelation 2:10

Christ's Letter to the Church in Smyrna

Let us look at the various elements of this exhortation:

Fear none of those things which come upon you: These words were spoken by Christ to the members of this church during their time of tribulation. He has not promised us that we would never suffer tribulation. Just the opposite is true. Our Lord has promised us tribulation:

In this world ye shall have tribulation.   John 16:33

We have nothing to fear, however. We are not the only ones who will suffer tribulations. Everyone on the face of the Earth must face them at one time or another. Job said:

Man that is born of a woman is of few days, and full of trouble.
                                                                    Job 14:1

Those who do not know Christ have only each other to cling to during their time of trouble, but we Christians not only have each other, we have Jesus. He has promised:

I will never leave thee, nor forsake thee. So that we may boldly say, the Lord is my helper, and I will not fear what man shall do unto me.   Hebrews 13:5-6

There is no fear in love; but perfect love casteth out fear: because fear hath torment. He that feareth is not made perfect in love.
                                                                    1 John 4:18

If we love and fear God, we need never fear man.
There will always be a strong bonding between Jesus and His believers because He faced every trial and tribulation we will ever encounter and was victorious. He said to us:

But be of good cheer; I have overcome the world.   John 16:33

When we face the things this world throws at us from time to time, we must remember that Jesus has already faced that problem and won. When His children are facing tribulation, He is always there to carry us through it.

THE WARNING

Behold, the devil shall cast some of you into prison, that ye may be tried; and ye shall have tribulation ten days.

Revelation 2:10

Let us examine the various elements of this warning:

Behold, the devil: Jesus labeled the devil as being the one responsible for the sufferings of the church at Smyrna. The Jews and Romans were just the instruments that the Devil used to bring about the persecutions, but we must remember that the Devil cannot do as he pleases. He is not the Almighty God. We learn from the book of Job that Satan has to get permission to do certain things to a child of God. When God gives His permission, it's for a reason. Now, God gives the reason that they will be cast into prison.

That ye might be tried: As we have seen, our faith and works for God will always be tried. Paul wrote to the Corinthians:

There hath no temptation taken you but such as is common to man: but God is faithful, who will not suffer you to be tempted above that ye are able; but will with the temptation also make a way to escape, that ye may be able to bear it.

1 Corinthians 10:13

Satan makes a big mistake when he decides to put God's children on trial. He must have regretted the serious indictment he brought against Job. God knew all along that Job would be faithful to Him, and when the trial was over Job was not only continuing to worship the Lord, but his material blessings had doubled.

Peter is another example. He was put into prison, and to make sure that he did not escape, extra guards were assigned to him and he was thrust into one of the innermost cells. The next morning the guards were still standing in their places and the prison doors were firmly locked, but Peter could not be found. An angel of the Lord had been sent to deliver him. Peter went straight to the place where he knew the members of the Church were praying. He wanted them to see that God had answered their prayers and given them a miracle.

Paul and Silas were beaten and thrown into prison in Philippi. Their feet and hands were secured in stocks. At midnight, however, they sang and praised God. When they did this, suddenly there was a great earthquake, and the foundations of the prison were shaken. Immediately the doors were opened and the prisoners were freed.

As a result of this miracle, the Philippian jailer and his family believed on the Lord Jesus and were baptized. A church was planted in that city. Satan had lost the battle again.

There are dozens of other examples in the Bible. Every time God's people are tried, He provides *"a way of escape"* so that we are *"able to bear it."*

Many things will soon come upon the Earth, but I want to encourage my fellow believers: *fear none of those things which thou shalt suffer.* Jesus will see us through whatever we might have to face.

Ye shall have tribulation ten days: Ten different Roman emperors brought persecution upon the early church, yet it survived and prospered.

THE PROMISE

Be thou faithful unto death and I will give thee a crown of life.
                                                        Revelation 2:10

A Christian must love Jesus more than his own life. When that is the case, Satan has no leverage over us. The Scriptures promise:

And they overcame him by the blood of the Lamb, and by the word of their testimony; and they loved not their lives unto the death.   Revelation 12:11

Our commitment to Christ is *"unto death,"* so death is no threat to us. When Jesus was about to raise Lazarus from the grave, He said to his sister Martha:

I am the resurrection, and the life: he that believeth in me, though he were dead, yet shall he live: John 11:25

Believers have passed from death unto life, and when we leave this world, we will just step out of this carnal body and into the very presence of God, where He has promised us *"a crown of life."* Why should we be worried about death? A perfect life was sacrificed so that the mess we make of our lives down here might be redeemed. I shudder to think of what sort of mess I might have made of things if Christ had not saved me forty-seven years ago. For all the redeemed a wonderful new world awaits. Let us be faithful unto death.

Christ's Letter to the Church in Smyrna

THE RELATIONSHIP BETWEEN THE IDENTITY AND THE MESSAGE

*And unto the angel of the church in Smyrna write; These things
saith the first and the last, which was dead, and is alive.*

Revelation 2:8

This is the way Jesus identified Himself to the second church
in Asia Minor, Smyrna, and to the second church era. Let us examine the various elements of this identity:

The first and the last: The Apostle John had this revelation. He
began the Gospel that bears his name with the words:

*In the beginning was the Word, and the Word was with God,
and the Word was God. The same was in the beginning with
God.* John 1:1-2

During the Revelation, Jesus also identified Himself to John
in another way:

*I am Alpha and Omega, the beginning and the ending, saith the
Lord, which is, and which was, and which is to come, the Almighty.* Revelation 1:8

Jesus wanted the Church to understand that He existed in the
beginning. He was God. God the Creator was the same Jesus
Christ who came to Earth incarcerated in a human body.

Which was dead: Although He was God, Jesus too had to face
death. He gave Himself up to die so that He could defeat death
and the grave. In the end, both death and the grave had to
release Him.

51

And is alive: Christ came out of the grave alive, but He also did something to death and the grave as He passed through them. He removed from them their sting for the child of God. Now, when a child of God dies, Jesus is there to meet them and usher them into His presence. Death is left a mere shadow of its former self. David was able to say:

Yea, though I walk through the valley of the shadow of death, I will fear no evil; for thou art with me.   Psalm 23:4

A shadow is as harmless as a hornet without a stinger or a dog without any teeth.

Jesus identified Himself in this manner, because He wants us to know that He died, but that He is alive and in control of our destinies. He personally takes charge of selecting those who will face martyrdom for Him and He has promised that He would not allow us to be tempted more than we could bear. I trust His judgment.

When Jesus was tried and sentenced to death, the Roman officials thought they were in control of things. Pilate had thought the same thing when Jesus stood before him. Jesus told him:

Thou couldest have no power at all against me, except it were given to thee from above.   John 19:11

The believers in the church in Smyrna were having to suffer many things, and Jesus wanted to reassure them. He did that in the way He identified Himself. He had been dead, but now He was alive. Everything that was happening to them was for a reason. He had allowed it to happen because they had given Him control of their lives. They felt that it was an honor to be chosen to be martyred for Jesus. Ignatius, one of the pastors of the Smyrna church during this time, wrote to the other churches requesting them not to pray for him to not be martyred. He wanted to face the Romans. He held no fear of death, and he got his wish. He was martyred giving praise to Jesus Christ.

Eusebius, the first Christian historian, lived during the time when the Christians were still under strong persecution. Elberhard Arnold, in his book *The Early Christians* (Baker Book House, 1979) records what Eusebius wrote about two early Christians, Carpus and Papylus, who were martyred. Before they were burned alive at the stake, he wrote, the proconsul ordered them to be hung up and have their skins flayed with tools of torture. Neither of them cried out in pain, but kept repeating over and over, "I am a Christian. I am a Christian." When they were nailed to the stake and burned alive, Papylus was first to be burned. When the flames leaped up he prayed quietly and gave up his soul. Carpus was nailed on next, and it could be seen that he was full of joy. When the fire was burning at its hottest, he was overheard to pray, "Praise be to thee, O Lord Jesus Christ, Son of God, that thou didst deem me, a sinner, also worthy of this part in thee." After he had said this, his soul departed from him.

A woman named Agathonica was present when these things happened. She saw the glory of God on Papylus and Carpus, and she cried out, "This meal has been prepared for me. I must partake in it. I must receive the meal of glory."

The people cried out, "Have mercy on your son."

Agathonica joyfully answered, "He has God who will care for him, for He is the Provider for us all. But I, why do I stand here?" She jubilantly allowed herself to be nailed to the stake. As she stood erect and caught on fire, she cried out three times, "Lord, Lord, Lord, help me, for I flee unto Thee."

I believe that our Lord Jesus Christ met these in the midst of their suffering and said to them, "See I told you that there was no reason to fear. I defeated death, and look, I am alive. I am the first, and I am the last. Enter into the joy of thy God. Receive your crown of life."

CHAPTER 4

CHRIST'S LETTER
TO THE CHURCH IN PERGAMUM

And to the angel of the church in Pergamos write; These things saith he which hath the sharp sword with two edges.

Revelation 2:12

This is the way Jesus identified Himself to the church in Pergamum. Later we will see how this identity relates to the message He sent to this church. The church in Pergamum represents the historical Church era from approximately 314 to 590 A.D.

THE CITY

Pergamum stood on the banks of the Caicus River, about twenty miles from the sea. The spot is now called Bergama. Ancient Pergamum was one of the most beautiful spots in Asia Minor. It was considered to be a royal city because it housed a temple built to honor Caesar Augustus. According to Hal Lindsey in his book, *There's A New World Coming* (Harvest House Publishers, 1984), each citizen of Pergamum was required to offer incense to the emperor once a year in that temple and to declare that the emperor was Lord. Caesar (100-44 B.C.) had his winter home in Pergamum, so he brought much financial gain to the city.

THE COMMENDATION

I know thy works, and where thou dwellest, even where Satan's seat is: and thou holdest fast my name, and hast not denied my faith, even in those days wherein Antipas was my faithful martyr, who was slain among you, where Satan dwelleth.

Revelation 2:13

Let us examine the various elements of this commendation:

I know thy works, and where thou dwellest, even where Satan's seat is: How good it is to know that Jesus is aware of everything we do for Him. Nothing goes unnoticed. Even the giving of a cup of cool water is recorded.

The people of this church were active for Jesus in spite of the fact that the city was given over to idolatry. Jesus knew where they lived, and He certainly knows where you and I live as well.

And thou holdest fast my name, and hast not denied my faith: Religion was big business in Pergamum, and Satan has set up his regional headquarters there. Many people think that Satan is only in Hell. That's not true. He is still right here on Earth. The Scriptures warn us:

Be sober, be vigilant; because your adversary the devil, as a roaring lion, walketh about, seeking whom he may devour.

1 Peter 5:8

While it is true that Satan will later be relegated to Hell (see Revelation 20:1-3), for the time being he is walking around right here, and you may even notice that he has set up a headquarters in your area.

The temple of Dionysius was also located in Pergamum. Dionysius was the same as Bacchus, the Roman god of wine and revelry. Dionysius is always depicted with his lower body being that of a goat and his upper body being that of a man. He has horns, cloven feet and a forked tail. This is, no doubt, where the idea got started that Satan had horns, cloven feet and a forked tail. Someone later added the pitchfork to top off this common caricature.

The Bible does not describe Satan in this manner at all. In fact, the Bible says:

And no marvel; for Satan himself is transformed into an angel of light.   2 Corinthians 11:14

Satan is a false angel of light and no wonder he gives people the deceitful impression that alcoholic beverages, drugs, sex outside of marriage, false religions and other such abominations are the way to a life of happiness.

There was another temple in Pergamum, the temple of Asklepios or Aesculapius. He was the patron god of the city and was considered to be the god of healing. In his temple a living serpent was the symbol of worship.

Healing in every imaginable form was practiced in this temple for both physical and psychological ailments. For instance, one of the cures was to place a sick person into the temple for the night and loose poisonous snakes to crawl over him. This may have been considered to be some sort of shock treatment. Who knows?

The Church of Pergamum was commended for holding fast the name of Jesus Christ. Despite the difficulty of their cultural circumstances, the people of faith remained true to their God.

One believer in Pergamum was Antipas. The only thing written of him was that he was "Christ's faithful martyr." Others paid a price for their faithfulness to Christ. The bishops Athanasius, Augustine, Jerome and others are remembered by history as having paid a great price to follow the Lord Jesus Christ.

THE REBUKE

But I have a few things against thee, because thou hast there them that hold the doctrine of Balaam, who taught Balac to cast a stumbling block before the children of Israel, to eat things sacrificed unto idols, and to commit fornication. So hast thou also them that hold the doctrine of the Nicolaitans, which thing I hate.
Revelation 2:14-15

Rebuke, when it comes from the Lord, is not a bad thing. When He rebukes, He does it with love and with the purpose of lifting us up. The Apostle Paul believed in rebuke and taught others to believe in its power. He wrote to Titus:

These things speak, and exhort, and rebuke with all authority.
Titus 2:15

Some of us resist rebuke, but when we know that the Lord Jesus rebukes for good, we should welcome His rebukes. Let us examine the various elements of this rebuke:

Thou hast there them that hold the doctrine of Balaam, who taught Balac to cast a stumblingblock before the children of Israel: This was the first thing Jesus was displeased about. Some in the church in Pergamum held to the doctrine of Balaam. Balaam taught Balac, the Moabite king, the way to corrupt Israel. It was to encourage intermarriage with the heathen by bringing desirable Moabite women into the camp of the people of Israel (see Numbers 31:15-16). The church of Pergamum allowed the unconverted to participate in the church, and just as the men of Israel had done in taking pagan women as their wives, this brought tragedy. The doctrine of Balaam then is what the Bible calls being unequally yoked with unbelievers. God's Word forbids it for our spiritual good:

Be ye not unequally yoked together with unbelievers: for what fellowship hath righteousness with unrighteousness? and what communion hath light with darkness? And what concord hath Christ with Belial? or what part hath he that believeth with an infidel? And what agreement hath the temple of God with idols? for ye are the temple of the living God; as God hath said, I will dwell in them, and walk in them; and I will be their God, and they shall be my people. Wherefore come out from among them, and be ye separate, saith the Lord, and touch not the unclean thing; and I will receive you. 2 Corinthians 6:14-17*

It was during this era of the church that Constantine made a union between church and the state. Unbelieving and unconverted people were suddenly being received into the church because it was now the state church. This was the beginning of Christianity without Christ, for it represents the same evil that corrupted Israel.

When the Israelite men married foreign women those women brought their pagan religions with them. We all know the power that the mother of the family exercises over her household. These pagan women were soon setting the standard of conduct in the land and the standards God had set for His people were lowered. Next came the idols and demonic worship, and soon Israel was in serious trouble with God.

The church faced this same struggle from the beginning of its existence, how to be friendly to the world in order to win the world to Christ while at the same time refraining from being unequally yoked with unbelievers. This is why Jesus said to the people of Pergamum, *"Thou hast there them that hold the doctrine of Balaam."*

To eat things sacrificed unto idols: The apostles had sent letters to all the churches informing them:

Abstain from pollutions of idols, and from fornication.

Acts 15:20

Until the year 313 A.D. every individual who desired to come into the fellowship of the Church had to learn the apostles' doctrine and pledge to follow its teachings before they were ever baptized in water or invited to partake of communion. Evidently some of the new members of the church in Pergamum had never heard of this order sent out by the apostles from Antioch, and they chose to consolidate Christianity with their traditional idol worship.

And to commit fornication: God hates fornication because it destroys families and it destroys churches. Faithfulness keeps families living together in harmony, but fornication (when a husband or wife breaks their vow to each other and commits adultery with another person) does harm to everyone concerned.

Faithfulness is just as important to the life of the Church. When a person repents and believes (casts himself upon) the Lord

Jesus Christ, he makes a commitment to Christ and to the Church to live for God. When we are unfaithful and untrustworthy, we have committed fornication against God and the Church.

The Church is committed to the Lord Jesus Christ to preach, teach, live and uphold His teachings. If the Church fails to fulfill this duty, it commits fornication against God. When a church has in its midst *"them that hold the doctrine of Balaam,... eat things sacrificed unto idols, and ... hold the doctrine of the Nicolaitans"* (which we will talk about next), this makes them fornicators because they are unfaithful to Jesus Christ the Lord.

So hast thou also them that hold the doctrine of the Nicolaitans, which thing I hate: Unlike the believers at Ephesus who hated this ungodly doctrine, there were some in the church at Pergamum that accepted it. These may well have been the same individuals who held to the doctrine of Balaam. As we have seen, the Nicolaitans reasoned that even though a person indulged in sins of the body, it did not defile his spirit. We still have people from both of these camps in our churches today. While they may be among us, they are not of us.

THE EXHORTATION

Repent.   Revelation 2:16

This is a command. Jesus hates to see His church lower her standards because it weakens the testimony of the entire Church. The Church must stand strong against false teachers and must unite against heresy.

From the time that Jesus sent the Holy Spirit into the Church on the Day of Pentecost in 33 A.D. until Constantine published the

Edict of Milan, granting freedom of religion in 313 A.D., many Christians were put to death for their faith. Some halfhearted church members were not ready to risk their lives or to be rejected by their friends and family.

When Constantine made the church official, all persecution ceased, and it actually became popular to be a Christian. After that, bishops often compromised their standards because of a celebrity figure who had joined them, a sad tendency that has remained a thorn in the side of the Church to this very day. The gate was thus opened for the unconverted to come into the Church. Many who had been excommunicated for denying Christ were reinstated.

Suddenly it was highly prestigious to be a bishop, when earlier the world had been crying out for their blood. And just as suddenly, the bishops turned from being humble, meek and faithful servants of Christ who were risking their lives daily to remain in the faith and became busy executives. Being elevated to such a high position since that time has often led men to compromise for the sake of politics.

I am sure that in the midst of the many fallen, there were still Christians who kept their eyes on Jesus and let nothing cause them to be proud or arrogant. They continued to praise and worship God in the beauty of holiness, knowing that it was only by the grace of God that their names were recorded in the Book of Life. Others who were carried away for a time by their new-found prestige no doubt later humbled themselves, repented and returned to an uncompromising position in the faith. Those who failed to repent formed another group that we will discuss later.

THE WARNING

Or else I will come unto thee quickly, and will fight against them with the sword of my mouth.　　　　　Revelation 2:16

Who are the *"them"* of this verse? They are:

1. Those who hold to the doctrine of Balaam.

These are unbelievers who are *in* the church but not *of* the church. They are the tares among the wheat, and it is sometimes difficult to distinguish them from the genuine believers.

2. Those who hold the doctrine of the Nicolaitians.

These are the ones who teach "take your freedom, and do what feels good," that it does not matter what one does in the body because what the body does never affects your spirit. The church at Ephesus had refused this doctrine, as did the church of the first era of church history, but it was later reintroduced.

As the Scriptures clearly show, God hates this doctrine, and those who believe the doctrine and fail to repent will have to fight against Him. When He takes action, it will be suddenly (quickly). Surely it is not wise to fight against God, and I would not like to be found in the shoes of those who try it.

THE PROMISE

To him that overcometh will I give to eat of the hidden manna, and will give him a white stone, and in the stone a new name written, which no man knoweth saving he that receiveth it.
Revelation 2:17

Let us examine the various elements of this promise:

To him that overcometh: It is possible for every believer to over-come the hypocrites and the sin-lovers among us. God has given us and them a chance to repent, and has commanded us to do so. Those who fail to do it in God's time will find that He does not accept their repentance. Now is the time to let Jesus into our hearts, and He will not come into an unrepentant heart. If we are to be overcomers, we all need His grace.

Will I give to eat of the hidden manna: This *"hidden manna"* is Jesus. The manna that God gave the children of Israel in the wilderness was a symbol of the body of Jesus Christ that was to be broken for the sins of the world. The reason it is called *"the hidden manna"* is because the earthly ministry of Jesus and His Church was hidden until it was revealed after His resurrection. We know this by the study of the Scriptures. Even His disciples did not know what He was talking about when He mentioned that He would go to Jerusalem and be put to death and the third day be raised from the grave. Peter even rebuked the Lord for saying such a thing.

From that time forth began Jesus to shew unto his disciples, how that he must go unto Jerusalem, and suffer many things of the elders and chief priests and scribes, and be killed, and be raised again the third day. Then Peter took him, and began to rebuke him, saying, Be it far from thee, Lord: this shall not be unto thee. But he turned, and said unto Peter, Get thee behind me, Satan: thou art an offence unto me: for thy savourest not the things that be of God, but those that be of men. Matthew 16:21-23

Earlier, Jesus had told His disciples that it was given unto them to know the mysteries of the Kingdom of God:

And he said unto them, Unto you it is given to know the mystery of the kingdom of God. Mark 4:11

After the resurrection, this mystery was revealed:

Now to him that is of power to stablish you according to my gospel, and the preaching of Jesus Christ, according to the revelation of the mystery, which was kept secret since the world began, But now is made manifest, and by the scriptures of the prophets, according to the commandment of the everlasting God, made known to all nations for the obedience of faith:
Romans 16:25-26

This Gospel is *"hidden manna"* because God, in His unlimited wisdom, has caused that those who care nothing for the Kingdom of God cannot find it. Only those who *"hunger and thirst after righteousness"* can be filled (Matthew 5:6). When the disciples asked Jesus why He spoke in parables, He told them plainly that it was to hide the truth from the insincere (see Matthew 13:10-17).

As I said, the manna that God gave the children of Israel in the wilderness was a symbol of the broken body of Jesus Christ. The Manna mentioned here in Revelation 2:17 is not a symbol. It is the real thing, and the promise given to the overcomers is that we will eat that *"hidden manna."* We become partakers of Christ's body. He said:

I am the bread of life: He that cometh to me shall never hunger; and he that believeth on me shall never thirst. John 6:35

And will give him a white stone, and in the stone a new name written, which no man knoweth saving he that receiveth it:
"A white stone" suggests that the believer is in close standing with Jesus (the Giver). It helped me to better understand this passage when I learned that the people of Asia Minor to whom

John was writing had a custom of giving to intimate friends what was known as "a 383." It was a cube or rectangular block of stone or ivory with words or symbols engraved on it. It was to be a secret, private possession of the one who received it. The "new name written" on the "white stone" may be a name that fits your born-again personality to perfection, the way Jesus sees you. It may be a pet name, very intimate, much like your parents would give you. It may also be a new name for Jesus, exactly what He meant to you. It would be unique for each of us, for He means something different to each one of us.

THE RELATIONSHIP BETWEEN THE IDENTITY AND THE MESSAGE

These things saith he which hath the sharp sword with two edges.
Revelation 2:12

This is the way Jesus identified Himself to the church in Pergamum and to the third church era. This "sharp sword" refers, of course, to the Word of God:

For the word of God is quick, and powerful, and sharper than any twoedged sword, piercing even to the dividing asunder of soul and spirit, and of the joints and marrow, and is a discerner of the thoughts and intents of the heart. Hebrews 4:12

And take ... the sword of the Spirit, which is the word of God.
Ephesians 6:17

That sharp, two-edged Sword can work for you or against you. One side is the grace of God, while the other side is the judgment of God. Both sides work to the advantage of the Church. On the grace side of the Sword are all the benefits offered to the Church. The judgment side of the Sword is used against the enemies of the Church. This statement is a warning to those who held the doctrine of Balaam and the doctrine of the Nicolaitans. God has just the right tool to separate them from His Church. The people of God's Church are not to be yoked to unbelievers and neither are they to continue living in sin. Some in the church in Pergamum and in the corresponding church era were guilty of both these violations.

The churches of Ephesus and Smyrna and their corresponding church eras hated both of these ungodly doctrines, and as we have seen, the Church, during these two periods, refused to serve communion to anyone until they had been taught the apostles' doctrine and been baptized in water. This common sense practice ceased in the Pergamum church era.

A lot more could be said about the Church lowering the standards of the Gospel during this period, but we don't want to deviate from the subject at hand here. Jesus was showing that the problem which existed in the Pergamum church and in the corresponding church age could be corrected by the proper teaching of the Word of God. Those that held to those doctrines could be judged by the Word as they faced the judgment side of that sharp two-edged Sword.

When the proper time comes the One with the Sword knows where to cut to separate those insincere people from the Church and the blessing of God and to mark them eternally as cut off. He knows the dividing line, and we will leave that to Him. Until that day comes, the messenger (pastor) of the church must use the sharp two-edged Sword (the Word of God) that has been given to us to bring believers into the Church and to cut the unbelievers out. The Word of God is the only answer to that problem.

With one side of the sword the messenger is to preach against sin. This side cuts and brings conviction and repentance. The other side of the sword is to be used by the messenger to exhort and edify the church to receive the grace of God. This sharp two-edged Sword is the only instrument the pastor has to bring people into a saving knowledge of Jesus Christ and to keep the church healthy, clean and undefiled.

When the Word of God is preached uncompromisingly in love it will do the work it was intended to do. The Holy Spirit uses that Word to invade the very thoughts and intents of our hearts. The process does the following:

1. Reproves us of sin, of righteousness and of judgment (see John 16:8)

2. Guides us into all truth (see John 16:13)

3. Shows us things to come (see John 16:13)

The messenger of the church (pastor) can accomplish nothing without the living (quick), powerful, sharp, piercing, dividing and discerning Word of God. This is where the Church gets it power. We will not get far in our prayer life unless we are in line with the Word of God. And if the Word of God is followed by the Church, the people who hold to the doctrine of Balaam and the doctrine of the Nicolaitans will have to repent or leave the church. If they refuse to listen to God's messengers, the time will come when God will use the Sword directly on them instead of by way of the messenger.

Another way this sharp Sword with two edges can work for the Church is in the area of physical and mental healing:

Even to the dividing asunder of soul and spirit, and ... joints and marrow. Hebrews 4:12

There is no part of our being that the Word of God is incapable of piercing. It reaches into every part of the body, the mind, the soul and the spirit. No one will ever invent an instrument that can compare to it. This sharp two-edged Sword can bring healing to every part of our beings.

In a future time, the same Spirit that raised Christ from the dead will quicken our mortal bodies, meaning it will raise us up from the grave (see Romans. 8:11). Each of us surely needs the One with the sharp two-edged sword to work for us.

What happens when the sharp two-edged Sword works against those who hold to the doctrine of Balaam and of the Nicolaitans? God told them to repent or He would come and fight against them *"with the sword of [His] mouth."* If those who hold to ungodly doctrines fail to repent, they must face the Lord Himself. They will not trouble the Church for long, for God Himself will deal with them. Their end will be tragic:

And to you who are troubled rest with us, when the Lord Jesus shall be revealed from heaven with his mighty angels, In flaming fire taking vengeance on them that know not God, and that obey not the gospel of our Lord Jesus Christ: Who shall be punished with everlasting destruction from the presence of the Lord, and from the glory of his power; 2 Thessalonians 1:7-9

It is a fearful thing to fall into the hands of the living God. Hebrews 10:31

And I saw heaven opened, and behold a white horse; and he that sat upon him was called Faithful and True, and in righteousness he doth judge and make war. His eyes were as a flame of fire, and on his head were many crowns; and he had a name written, that no man knew, but he himself. And he was clothed with a vesture

69

dipped in blood: and his name is called The Word of God. And the armies which were in heaven followed him upon white horses, clothed in fine linen, white and clean. And out of his mouth goeth a sharp sword, that with it he should smite the nations: and he shall rule them with a rod of iron: and he treadeth the winepress of the fierceness and wrath of Almighty God. And he hath on his vesture and on his thigh a name written, KING OF KINGS, AND LORD OF LORDS.   Revelation 19:11-16

CHAPTER 5

CHRIST'S LETTER TO THE CHURCH IN THYATIRA

And unto the angel of the church in Thyatira write; These things saith the Son of God, who hath his eyes like unto a flame of fire, and his feet are like fine brass.   Revelation 2:18

As He had with the other churches, Jesus identified Himself to the church in Thyatira. He let the believers there know who it was that was talking to them. It was, He said, the very *Son of God.* Then He added the phrase *"who hath his eyes like unto a flame of fire and his feet are like fine brass."* Both of these latter identities symbolize judgment. The church in Thyatira represents the period in church history that has come to be called the Dark Ages. It extended from about 590-1517 A.D. and was a time when many false practices crept into and contaminated the church.

THE CITY

Leaving the city of Pergamum and moving inland, Thyatira was situated in the mouth of a long valley connecting two other valleys, Hermus and Caicos. Built for defense, the city itself stood in the middle of this vale on a slight rise. As extra security for the city, the Romans stationed their elite guards there.

The main industry of Thyatira was cloth dyeing and the specialty of the city was cloth dyed in beautiful red and purple shades. The purple colors were called "Turkey red," and the dye for them was taken from a plant that grew in that area. This plant and the dye the locals extracted from it made the people of Thyatira famous throughout the Roman Empire. Lydia, a seller of this famous purple cloth, which was so well known that it came to be called simply "purple," was the first convert in Thyatira (see Acts 16:14-15).

According to history there were many trade guilds in the city of Thyatira, and it was difficult to do business there without belonging to one of those guilds. This created a problem for those who accepted Christ because paganism and immorality was a way of life in the guilds.

In Thyatira, there were other elements of paganism. There was a temple for fortune-tellers with a female oracle presiding over it. Apollo, the Roman sun god, was worshipped there as well. The locals called him Tyrimnos. Altogether, it was not an atmosphere conducive to the Christian faith.

THE COMMENDATION

I know thy works, and charity, and service, and faith, and thy patience, and thy works; and the last to be more than the first.
Revelation 2:19

There were true believers in the church in Thyatira and in the church of the Dark Ages. Like Israel, the Church has always had its faithful followers, even when many or most have turned away from the true God and His ways.

God has never been without what the Bible calls *"a remnant."* Despite the wickedness of Ahab and Jezebel in turning Israel to idolatry, Elijah stood faithful to God and found that seven thousand others had also not bowed their knee to Baal (see 1 Kings 19:18). Even when the people of Israel were taken into captivity, there were still those among them who remained true believers. These were men of strong faith, like Jeremiah, Ezekiel, Isaiah, Daniel, the four Hebrew children and many others who were not specifically mentioned by name in the Bible narrative. Israel had her faithful men and women and so did the Church, even in its darkest hour.

Let us now look at the various elements of this commendation:

I know thy works: The church in Thyatira was to be commended for its faithfulness to God even while many of their leaders were compromising their faith to join the worldly elite. Satan has never been successful, nor will he ever be, in destroying Israel or the Church of the Lord Jesus Christ. There will always be true believers who will work for their Lord. Paul showed us that we were *"created in Christ Jesus unto good works"* (Ephesians 2:10). People of true faith refuse to let backsliders discourage them. They go on serving their Lord regardless of what others do. Jesus said:

Let your light so shine before men, that they may see your good works, and glorify your Father which is in heaven.
Matthew 5:16

And love: Despite the fact that the leaders of the church in Thyatira and in the corresponding church age lowered their standards and substituted ritualism for the Word of God, the faithful still loved Jesus Christ and each other. Church history confirms this. It mentions such God-loving saints as: Bernard of Clairvaux, Peter Waldo, John Wycliff, John Huss and

Savonarole. Every one of these men refused to depart from the true faith of Jesus Christ. As Paul wrote to the Corinthians:

Charity [love] never faileth.   1 Corinthians 13:8

And faith: That believers in the church in Thyatira had love and faith is shown by the works they performed. Paul wrote of *"faith which worketh by love"* (Galatians 5:6). This church had three things that God expects from all of us: love and faith and the works which such love and faith produce. When the Scriptures speak of great men and women of faith (Hebrews 11), their faith is shown by their acts. Abel's faith is shown in the sacrifice he offered, Noah's faith is shown in the ark he built, and Abraham's faith is shown in the journey he made. That pattern of faith and works is repeated over and over throughout the Scriptures. The faithful in Thyatira also put their love and faith into action.

And thy works: For a second time Jesus mentioned works in this letter. During this church era, men like John Wycliff translated the Bible into a language that the people could read for themselves. He and others like him were martyred for their faith and their good works.

And the last to be more than the first: Our works of faith must never take a back seat to anything. If the works are not there, faith is also absent. As this particular church period went on, there arose a greater and greater hunger for the Word of God, and as the faithful servants of the Lord published His Word (under the threat of death), the people of the church were inspired to greater and greater works. This is as it should be.

Christ's Letter to the Church in Thyatira

THE REBUKE

Notwithstanding I have a few things against thee, because thou sufferest that woman Jezebel, which calleth herself a prophetess, to teach and to seduce my servants to commit fornication, and to eat things sacrificed unto idols. Revelation 2:20

In Thyatira, an occult prophetess was given liberties within the church and this deceived many of the people. This woman was believed to have been the chief oracle of that large shrine for occult mediums and fortune-tellers in the city. We even know her name: Sambathe. Jesus saw her as a "Jezebel." Just as Jezebel, the pagan wife of King Ahab, had led the children of Israel into the worship of Baal during her time, Sambathe, the heathen prophetess, seduced the people of Thyatira. Jezebel's worship of Baal had been mixed with debased sexual acts and Sambathe also convinced her followers to mix idolatry and sexual impurity with their Christianity.

It was during the Dark Ages that the church introduced the worship of saints and images and relics, and these are nothing more than idols. Worship, which in the early Church, was spontaneous and vibrant, now degenerated into dry ritual. As the leaders of the church drew back from the Word of God as the source of enlightenment and substituted their own teachings, intimacy with God was sacrificed.

When we bow to anything or anyone other than God, it is an act of spiritual fornication. When the people of Israel were found to be worshipping idols, God likened them to Hosea's wife, Gomer, a woman of whoredoms. And God has not changed His opinion in this regard.

When Christians take on that name, the name of Christ, they become married to Him. Therefore, bowing before another is an act of unfaithfulness that creates a serious breach in the relationship. We are called to worship Him only.

THE EXHORTATION

But unto you I say, and unto the rest in Thyatira, as many as have not this doctrine, and which have not known the depths of Satan, as they speak; I will put upon you none other burden.
Revelation 2:24

Let us examine the various elements of this exhortation:

But unto you I say, and unto the rest in Thyatira, as many as have not this doctrine: Jesus was now speaking to the others, those who did not have the doctrine of Jezebel. There have always been people in every church and in every church age who have known the voice of the Shepherd and will not follow a stranger (Satan's servants). The Lord has something more to say to those of us who have taken this course:

Which have not known the depths of Satan: The Greek word translated here as "depths" is *bathus*. It means the same as profound or deep as in "intellectually deep," or "learned." We are not destined to know the depths of Satan, to be learned in his ways. When our children are young, we teach them to fear a rattlesnake and tell them that rattlesnakes are dangerous. "Don't ever play with snakes," we warn them. There may come a time when our children will have to deal with a snake, but it would be dangerous to allow them to be charmed by a serpent.

It is wrong to play with the things of the devil. In Jesus' day, He didn't play with demons. He cast them out. He taught the apostles to cast them out and commanded us to cast them out as well. Several years ago, a demon possessed lady came into our Church office. Nothing she said made sense, but she insisted on rattling on and on. Sensing that we were getting nowhere, I said, "Shut up, you demon, and listen to me. Get out of this woman and don't you ever return!"

The puzzled look vanished from the woman's face, and she said, "I feel sleepy." My wife told her to just stretch out on the couch and sleep. Later, when she awoke, she asked, "Where am I?" We told her where she was and what had happened. She was very embarrassed by some of the things she said and didn't remember it at all. She was totally delivered and years later she was still free.

But this is not child's play. Don't ever take the devil lightly or play around with him or his ways. Only learn enough about him to keep him at arm's length. The fascination we see in many for everything satanic is dangerous. My cry is that of St. Paul:

That I may know him, and the power of his resurrection, and the fellowship of his sufferings, being made conformable unto his death. Philippians 3:10

Some people who are engaged in the deliverance ministry (and I believe that God gave it to them) have nothing but demons on their mind all the time. Our attention must be on Jesus. He wants first place in our hearts, in our minds and in our souls. Jesus is as jealous of our attention as we are with our spouses. I know there are other men in this world, but I don't want my wife thinking about them all the time. In the same way, Jesus wants our thoughts to be continually of Him. Paul wrote to the Philippians:

Finally, brethren, whatsoever things are true, whatsoever things are honest, whatsoever things are just, whatsoever things are pure, whatsoever things are lovely, whatsoever things are of good report; if there be any virtue, and if there be any praise, think on these things. Philippians 4:8

There are many things about Satan that I have no desire to know because they are only learned by experience. I don't know how it feels to be in prison, and I don't want to know how it feels. I don't know how it feels to be a drug addict, to be an abuser, to be a murderer or to be in deep depression and I have no desire to know.

Concerning Satan, the Scriptures teach us:

• Not to be ignorant of his devices
• That he has no power against the name of Jesus Christ
• That we should use the gift of discerning of spirits to know what he is up to
• That we should resist him and that when we do, he will flee from us
• That we should draw near to God and let God draw near to us

If God did not include a deep knowledge of Satan and his ways in the teaching of the Bible, it is because we have no need to know it, so why should we seek it outside the Bible?

As they speak: This phrase might be translated "or so they boast." Some of the Thyatirans were so deceived by the "prophetess" and her followers that they were boasting about knowing the depths of Satan's mysteries. The Lord was not at all impressed with them.

I will put upon you none other burden: Our Lord Jesus Christ is wonderful. He never puts more on His children than is necessary. This same statement was made by the apostles when they sent a letter to all the churches of their period, refusing to force Christians to obey the law of circumcision. What God tells us is good for us, or He would not tell us about it at all.

THE WARNING

And I gave her space to repent of her fornication; and she repented not. Behold, I will cast her into a bed, and them that commit adultery with her into great tribulation, except they repent of their deeds. And I will kill her children with death; and all the churches shall know that I am he which searcheth the reins and hearts: and I will give unto every one of you according to your works. But unto you I say, and unto the rest in Thyatira, as many as have not this doctrine, and which have not known the depths of Satan, as they speak; I will put upon you none other burden. But that which ye have already hold fast till I come.

Revelation 2:21-25

Let us examine the various elements of this warning:

And I gave her space to repent of her fornication; and she repented not: Behold, I will cast her into a bed, and them that commit adultery with her into great tribulation, except they repent of their deeds: This woman Sambathe, the *"Jezebel"* of Thyatira, was given an opportunity to repent, but she refused. God did not destroy her, but He cast her into a bed, a sign of helplessness, and those who committed adultery with her, He said, would find themselves in *"great tribulation"* — *"except they repent of their deeds."* Sin never goes unpunished. If it is not repented of, it brings helplessness and *"great tribulation."*

79

And I will kill her children with death: Innocent children pay the biggest price when their parents commit adultery and fornication, whether it is physical or spiritual. When trust in broken in the home, it becomes a war zone, and children are caught in the crossfire.

It is difficult to describe the scene of battle. Nerves are shattered, dreams are destroyed and all thought of unity for the common good vanishes. This is the breeding ground for dropping out of school, experimentation with alcohol, drugs and sex and the doorway to crime. Helplessness is a good expression for it. It is a death sentence for the family.

In the fourth church age, spiritual fornication became rampant. God gave the people of the church opportunity to repent and to abandon their idols and dead rituals, but, for the most part, they refused. The Jezebel spirit had so taken hold of their lives that they could not bear to let it go.

The physical church prospered until one church leader was reported to have boasted, "No longer do we have to say like Peter, 'Silver and gold have I none.' "

Someone was heard to answer, "But neither can we say to the crippled, 'Rise up and walk.' "

Today, in the place where the great city of Thyatira once stood proud and tall, there is no Christian church. Moslem law even forbids the preaching of the Gospel there. For those citizens who may be descendants of the very Christians who received this letter from Jesus, the prophecy has come to pass: *"I will kill her children with death."*

And all the churches shall know: What an interesting statement! True Christians have a deep love for God and for His Word. Jesus knew that we would be searching the Scriptures in our day and that we would see how He related to man in past generations. The more we search the Word of God and the more prayerfully we search the Word of God, the more we see His perfection and the perfection of His Word. Looking back, we know that He searched the hearts of those church members, and we can know that He is doing the same with us. As we study church history and learn what happened to other churches and other periods, we can see that Jesus Christ was faithful to fulfill every warning and every promise that He made. We now know as He said we would.

I am he which searcheth the reins and hearts: This statement should never be taken lightly. Let us keep it uppermost in our minds at all times. It is an easy one to forget. When we become successful at something, we too easily equate that with the blessing of God, and that may not always be true. Some churches grow very rapidly, but God is looking for more than numbers. The Pharisees had numbers. God is looking for quality of heart among His people. Jesus spoke of a people whose heart had *"waxed gross"* (Matthew 13:15). When it happened, He said, their ears become *"dull of hearing"* and their eyes *"closed."*

Pastors, church staff members, and Christians of every level must guard their hearts. We must all keep a pure, hungry, obedient and open heart to God, so that the Holy Spirit can cause us to know the things we need to know. Only then can we serve God with full assurance and without any condemnation. As John wrote to the churches:

And hereby we know that we are of the truth, and shall assure our hearts before him. For if our heart condemn us, God is greater than our heart, and knoweth all things. Beloved, if our heart condemn us not, then have we confidence toward God.

1 John 3:19-21

And he that overcometh: This condition had to be met by every believer in every one of the seven churches, and in every church of every age. Satan uses this world with all its materialistic attractions, what the Bible calls *"the lust of the flesh, and the lust of the eyes, and the pride of life"* (1 John 2:16) to attract us away from God. We must desire God more than we desire the things of this world if we are to overcome.

There is only one way to overcome the world. John wrote:

For whatsoever is born of God overcometh the world: and this is the victory that overcometh the world, even our faith. Who is he that overcometh the world, but he that believeth that Jesus is the Son of God? 1 John 5:4-5

When I believed on Jesus Christ and received Him into my heart in 1952, I was born again. My desires changed, and so did my life. Such a wonderful thing happened in my life that I was sure I would never sin again. I was wrong. Despite my noblest efforts, I still fell short of God's expectations.

I immediately overcame the major sins, like gambling and cursing, but there was so much more I needed to learn. I was still impatient at times, had a hard time turning the other cheek when I was provoked, had to learn to resist the temptation to discouragement and to being judgmental. That all took more time. In spite of my weaknesses, however, I never lost faith in Jesus, and I went on to overcome in others areas of my life. I'm still not perfect, but I'm working on it.

There are still many flaws in us, thinking of ourselves before others, being touchy and fretful and worrying for example, but the Holy Spirit of God is at work in our lives, rooting out every evil thought and action. I, like Paul, know that I must attain unto the resurrection of the dead:

Christ's Letter to the Church in Thyatira

If by any means I might attain unto the resurrection of the dead. Not as though I had already attained, either were already perfect: but I follow after, if that I may apprehend that for which also I am apprehended of Christ Jesus. Brethren, I count not myself to have apprehended: but this one thing I do, forgetting those things which are behind, and reaching forth unto those things which are before, I press toward the mark for the prize of the high calling of God in Christ Jesus. Philippians 3:11-14

Through Christ we will indeed overcome. He promises:

I can do all things through Christ which strengtheneth me.
Philippians 4:13

But that which ye have already hold fast till I come: The Lord did not tell the people of the church at Thyatira that they did not have anything. They had something and they needed to hold onto that something until the end. We could say this same thing about churches and about most believers. We all have some good things that we must cling to, and there are some other things we would best lay aside. As the writer of the letter to the Hebrews declared:

Let us lay aside every weight, and the sin which doth so easily beset us. Hebrews 12:1

THE PROMISE

And he that overcometh, and keepeth my works unto the end, to him will I give power over the nations: And he shall rule them with a rod of iron; as the vessels of a potter shall they be broken to shivers: even as I received of my Father. And I will give him the morning star. He that hath an ear, let him hear what the Spirit saith unto the churches.   Revelation 2:26-29

Let us examine the various elements of this promise:

And he that overcometh, and keepeth my works unto the end:
To be an overcomer is not an option. It is a must. God does not accept wavering faith. James wrote:

He that wavereth is like a wave of the sea driven with the wind and tossed. For let not that man think that he shall receive any thing of the Lord.   James 1:6-7

Jesus spoke of those who would keep His works *"unto the end."* He did some powerful and wonderful things to save us and to give us all the benefits of Calvary. We must never lose faith in His works. Keep it *"unto the end."* Be faithful to Him *"unto the end."*

To him will I give power over the nations: Those who overcome may not necessarily have a high position here on Earth, but they will surely rank high in the Kingdom of God. Jesus said that all power *"in heaven and in earth"* had been given to Him:

All power is given unto me in heaven and in earth.
          Matthew 28:18

Since all power has been given to the Lord, it is His to delegate as He wishes. Surely He would not appoint a quitter to a high position of authority in the Kingdom. There are great things for us to do, as we shall see. Paul wrote:

Do ye not know that the saints shall judge the world?
1 Corinthians 6:2

And he shall rule them with a rod of iron, as the vessels of a potter shall they be broken to shivers [pieces]: even as I received of my Father: This is in reference to the Millennial reign of Christ which He will share with His Church. The form of government in that day will not be democratic, but theocratic, which means that it will be under God's control. Satan has had his chance to govern the world, and man has had his. The result has been total chaos. When Christ returns, the vessels of the potter shall be broken to shivers (pieces). King David prophesied this:

Ask of me, and I shall give thee the heathen for thine inheritance, and the uttermost parts of the earth for thy possession. Thou shalt break them with a rod of iron; thou shalt dash them in pieces like a potter's vessel. Psalm 2:8-9

We are blessed to have the opportunity to rule with Christ for a thousand years on this Earth and to reign with Him forever in the New Heaven and New Earth. This is exciting, but there is much more to come.

And I will give him the morning star: This star represents Christ and an appointed time. He is the bright and morning star (see Revelation 22:16). At the appointed time, He will come and banish all darkness by His bright shining. Peter wrote,

We have also a more sure word of prophecy; whereunto ye do well that ye take heed, as unto a light that shineth in a dark place, until the day dawn, and the day star arise in your hearts. 2 Peter 1:19

God requires that we keep our faith strong and steadfast in Him if we expect to overcome in this sin-infested world. Those who meet God's requirements will be given *"the Morning Star,"* and that Morning Star is Jesus, the light of the world.

THE RELATIONSHIP BETWEEN THE IDENTITY AND THE MESSAGE

These things saith the Son of God, who hath his eyes like unto a flame of fire, and his feet are like fine brass.   Revelation 2:18

This is the way Jesus identified Himself to the church at Thyatira and to the fourth church era. Let us examine the various elements of this identity:

The Son of God: When a father has to speak to his children, they take notice. They know it is time to shape up and put things right. It is time to focus our attention on the Son of God, not on the saints of bygone days. Jesus said:

I am the way, the truth, and the life: no man cometh unto the Father, but by me.   John 14:6

Paul wrote to Timothy:

For there is one God, and one mediator between God and men, the man Christ Jesus.   1 Timothy 2:5

The commendations of these letters, the rebukes, the exhortations, the warnings and the promises are from the Son of God, and from none other. They are not even from the apostles or the prophets. Christ identified Himself as the Source of all power in Heaven and in Earth.

Christ's Letter to the Church in Thyatira

Who hath eyes like unto a flame of fire, and his feet are like fine brass: Jesus was grieved by the unfaithfulness of many, by the lowering of standards in the church in general and by the fact that many had yoked themselves up with unbelievers. Their spiritual fornication broke His heart. Jezebel was among them.

Contrary to what some teach, it is important to please God, to walk in a way that brings joy to His heart. If we insist on ignoring His Word, we will surely reap the consequences. Some people have tried very hard to present Jesus as a figure voice of authority. While it is true that He is love, it is also true that He is the Great Judge. While it is true that He is the meek lamb of God, when He comes again it will be as "The Lion of the tribe of Judah" (Revelation 5:5). He is both Savior and Judge, both Lamb and Lion.

When Jesus went to visit His hometown of Nazareth, He was invited to stand and read the weekly scripture lesson. He was handed the scroll of Isaiah and He opened it to Isaiah 61. There He read Isaiah's prophecy of the Savior's coming. The people were captivated as He read those powerful words that day:

The spirit of the Lord GOD is upon me; because the LORD hath anointed me to preach good tidings unto the meek; he hath sent me to bind up the brokenhearted, to proclaim liberty to the captives, and the opening of the prison to them that are bound; To proclaim the acceptable year of the LORD ... .   Isaiah 61:1-2

He closed the book, gave it back to the minister and sat down. But He had not finished the verse. The rest of it read:

... and the day of vengeance of our God.

Isaiah 61:2

I believe the reason Jesus did this was that His first coming would be one of grace. In this advent He would demonstrate *"the acceptable year of the Lord."* That did not mean that *"the day of vengeance of our God"* would never come. It was for another time and will be accomplished when Christ returns.

The story is told of a young man who had committed a crime. The lawyer that defended him in court was very effective. He won the case and the young man went free. The young man continued his life of crime and some years later he was arrested and charged with murder. When he was brought before the judge, he was encouraged to see that it was the very lawyer who had defended him on the previous occasion. His hopes for acquittal rose. The judge, however, found the man guilty and sentenced him to death for his crimes.

As the sentence was pronounced, the man cried out, "I'm Harry! Don't you remember me? I am the one you defended and I was acquitted."

"Yes, I do remember," replied the judge, "I was your defender then, but I am your judge now."

Jesus is our Defender now, but if our faith is not strong enough to endure to the end, He will be our Judge in the Day of Vengeance.

CHAPTER 6

CHRIST'S LETTER
TO THE CHURCH IN SARDIS

And unto the angel of the church in Sardis write; These things saith he that hath the seven Spirits of God, and the seven stars; I know thy works, that thou hast a name that thou livest, and art dead. Revelation 3:1

This is the way Jesus indentified Himself to the church in Sardis. This church is representative of the church era of approximately 1517-1900 A.D. This includes the Reformation period. Although the Reformation gave rise to forceful revival movements, the resulting churches often quickly fell into formalism and denominational squabbling.

THE CITY

Sardis was located inland and built on a small elevated plateau which rose sharply above the Hermus Valley. Five hundred years before John received the revelation of this letter to the church there, Sardis was one of the most powerful and one of the richest cities of the known world. In 17 A.D., Sardis was leveled by an earthquake, and although it was rebuilt by Tiberius Caesar, it never regained its original state of power and wealth.

Sardis was also infected with paganism. The people worshipped in the double temples of Cybele and Apollo, Cybele being the goddess of the moon and Apollo, the god of the sun. They were said to be brother and sister.

THE COMMENDATION

I know thy works. Revelation 3:1

"Works" seems to have been about the only thing this church had going for it, and even the works, when carefully examined, were not found to be perfect before God.

Many years ago I preached in a church that needed a pastor. That church had a lot going for it. The building was large and beautiful. The members were financially secure and held high positions in the community. The new pastor would be handsomely rewarded with a fine salary. But I would not have pastored that church for anything. It was spiritually dead. Sardis must have been like that.

THE REBUKE

That thou hast a name that thou livest, and art dead.
Revelation 3:1

At one time Sardis could boast of an alive church. People were being saved. Their lives were being touched and changed. In the services, they were being inspired and healed. Now, however, they seemed to be running on their past record. This is unacceptable. Any church that is not close to God NOW is in trouble. The Bible has a name for people who are not as close to God as they once were, and it is not a pleasant name: BACKSLIDER.

There are backslidden people and there are backslidden churches. Backsliders become hardened to God and hardened to

His Word. They are cold and stiff. Their vision for lost souls is gone. Their joy is gone. Their spontaneity in praise is gone. They need revival.

The story is told of a note that was found on the pew of a church. It read, "This church is as cold as the coldest wind that ever blew, and in its pews is but a few. You will all be hot before I return."

If something is dead, it is vain to go on pretending that it is alive. Some people will paste a dead smile on their face and go to church week after week. Even preachers do it. They preach one way and live another. But regardless of the false front we may put on, God knows the truth. We may be able to sustain ourselves for a time on the reputation of once being alive, but if we are dead, that fact will sooner or later become common knowledge. Just as surely as God knows it, people will soon know it too.

THE EXHORTATION

Be watchful, and strengthen the things which remain, that are ready to die: for I have not found thy works perfect before God. Remember therefore how thou hast received and heard, and hold fast, and repent.   Revelation 3:2-3

Let us examine the various elements of this exhortation:

Be watchful: The people of Sardis knew what Jesus meant by this phrase. Because Sardis was located on the top of a mountain and there was only one opening into the city, guards were kept at this location. The people of the city felt very secure, but the sense of security was misplaced. Over time the guards, who by now were not expecting any trouble, grew accustomed to sleeping at their post. According to Dr. J. Vernon McGee in his *Through the Bible with J. Vernon McGee*, one night in 218

B.C. while the guards slept, enemies entered the city and sacked it.

After that night, the citizens of Sardis understood the need to *"be watchful."* This is a lesson every believer must learn. Satan, our deadly enemy, never sleeps. He is always looking for an opening, an opportunity, a moment of laxness on our part. Because of the years of relative peace and prosperity through which we have passed, the Church has become far too complacent. It is easy to do. If we don't regularly study God's Word, pray, practice holiness and stay in fellowship with other Christians, we can quickly become lax. When Jesus prophesied about the end-times, the word He kept repeating over and over again was *"WATCH."*

Strengthen the things which remain, that are ready to die: The guards at Sardis could not strengthen their weakened barriers if they were asleep. Sleeping during a time of responsibility is a sign of an uncaring attitude or the result of false security. Satan will take advantage of every opportunity we give him. Paul wrote to the Corinthian believers:

Wherefore let him that thinketh he standeth take heed lest he fall.
1 Corinthians 10: 12

There is nothing more valuable than your eternal salvation. That is why God's Word warns us:

Wherefore the rather, brethren, give diligence to make your calling and election sure:　　　　2 Peter 1:10

Remember therefore how thou hast received and heard, and hold fast: I read a story many years ago that I never forgot. A certain church had grown cold and indifferent toward God. Little by little all the members left the church, until an elderly lady found herself alone each time she went for service. She never missed a service. Never mind that the pastor was gone, the choir was gone, the people were gone. She would kneel in prayer, worship and read her Bible. After this had gone on for quite a while, one day another believer joined her, then another and another, until the church was again overflowing and on fire for God. God sent a good pastor to shepherd that flock. I thank God for people like that little lady. Her garments were not defiled, and she strengthened that which remained. She held fast to that which she had received and heard, and God sent an increase. We would all do well to follow her example.

THE WARNING

If therefore thou shalt not watch, I will come on thee as a thief, and thou shalt not know what hour I will come upon thee.
Revelation 3:3

Jesus told the story of the ten virgins, five of them foolish and five of them wise (see Matthew 25:1-13). What happened to the five foolish virgins is exactly what happened to the church in Sardis. When the Bridegroom came, they were unprepared. It never pays to have an uncaring attitude or a false security. Check your heart today. Make sure that you are keeping the faith.

When the Apostle Paul checked his heart, he was able to declare:

I have fought a good fight, I have finished my course, I have kept the faith.   2 Timothy 4:7

How about you?

THE PROMISE

He that overcometh, the same shall be clothed in white raiment; and I will not blot out his name out of the book of life, but I will confess his name before my Father, and before his angels.
Revelation 3:5

Let us look at the various elements of this promise:

He that overcometh: Here it is again, this word overcome. Jesus Christ made this same statement to every one of the seven churches in Asia Minor. We don't hear this word nearly enough in our pulpits these days. Another one we need to hear more often is a word the disciples used a lot: endure. This concept of overcoming, enduring, was strongly taught by the bishops who had been ordained and trained by the original apostles in the early church. When Justin Martyr was asked, just before he was martyred for his faith in Christ, "Do you believe that when you are put to death that you will have everlasting life and be with Jesus Christ?" he eagerly answered, "If I keep the faith and endure to the end, I shall live with my Lord eternally." Since this is a such key issue in our Lord's letters to the churches, we will deal with it in more detail later.

The same shall be clothed in white raiment: White is a symbol for purity. The white raiment of the saints is the wedding garment of the Bride of Jesus. It is a symbol of the righteousness of Christ. When we are clothed in the righteousness of Jesus Christ, which is the meaning of "clothed in white raiment," God no longer sees our failures (sin). He only sees the purity of His Son Jesus Christ in which we are clothed. If we had to appear before God in our own righteousness, we would, of course, be dressed in filthy rags.

And I will not blot out his name out of the book of life, but I will confess his name before my Father, and before his angels: Jesus has promised those who are overcomers that they would be dressed in white raiment, that He would not blot their name out of the Book of Life, and that He would confess their name before the Father, and before His angels. This means that you and I are a part of the Body of Jesus, the Church (His Bride). When Jesus confesses our name before His Father and before His holy angels, He is talking about a wedding. He would never yoke Himself to an unfaithful Bride as the church of Pergamum did. He would never marry a Jezebel, as the church of Thyatira did. He will yoke Himself to a pure and faithful Bride, one made clean by His blood. As she follows Him, she will become more and more like Him:

But we all, with open face beholding as in a glass the glory of the Lord, are changed into the same image from glory to glory, even as by the Spirit of the Lord. 2 Corinthians 3:18

The Spirit of the Lord is tutoring His Bride. She must conform to His image, and in order to do that she must overcome Satan and this world. Dear friend, don't think that you can be conformed to the world and wear white raiment and have Jesus confess you, saying I do take _(put your name here)_ as my Bride, before my Father, and before His Angels. Jesus is coming for a spotless Bride:

That he might present it to himself a glorious church, not having spot, or wrinkle, or any such thing; but that it should be holy and without blemish. Ephesians 5:27

When we really love Jesus, we make Him Lord of our lives. Some desperately want Jesus to be their Savior, but they are not willing for Him to be their Lord. Personally, I don't believe it will work. Every promise that Jesus makes to the Church is based on the condition that we be overcomers. Every church that received a rebuke from the Lord also received a warning. If we take His warnings seriously, then we must give heed to them. There are serious consequences to a failure to repent. To Ephesus, He said:

Do the first works; or else I will come unto thee quickly, and will remove thy candlestick out of his place, EXCEPT THOU RE-PENT.   Revelation 2:5

To Pergamum, He said:

REPENT; or else I will come unto thee quickly, and will fight against them with the sword of my mouth.   Revelation 2:16

To Thyatira, He said:

And I gave her space to repent of her fornication; and she repented not. Behold, I will cast her into a bed, and them that commit adultery with her into great tribulation, EXCEPT THEY RE-PENT of their deeds. And I will kill her children with death; and all the churches shall know that I am he which searcheth the reins and hearts: and I will give unto every one of you according to your works.   Revelation 2:21-23

To Sardis, He said:

Remember therefore how thou hast received and heard, and hold fast, and REPENT. If therefore thou shalt not watch, I will come on thee as a thief, and thou shalt not know what hour I will come upon thee. Revelation 3:3

And to the Laodiceans and their era, He said:

So then because thou art lukewarm, and neither cold nor hot, I will spue thee out of my mouth. Because thou sayest, I am rich, and increased with goods, and have need of nothing; and knowest not that thou art wretched, and miserable, and poor, and blind, and naked. Revelation 3:16-17

From these letters to the churches, I am convinced that those who fail to overcome will take their place with the apostate church. Here is my reasoning:

1. Jesus will not fight against His Church and He said, *"Repent; or else I will come unto thee quickly, and will fight against them with the sword of my mouth"* (Revelation 2:16). He has promised to fight our battle (see 2 Chronicles 20:17). He does not fight against us.

2. The Church of the Lord Jesus Christ is not a fornicator, and He would not kill her children, yet He said, *"And I gave her space to repent of her fornication; and she repented not. Behold, I will cast her into a bed, and them that commit adultery with her into great tribulation, except they repent of their deeds. And I will kill her children with death"* (Revelation 2:21-23). He promised to save our households (see Acts 16:31), not destroy them.

3. Jesus would not come upon His church as a thief, yet He said, *"Repent. If therefore thou shalt not watch, I will come on thee as a*

thief, and thou shalt not know what hour I will come upon thee" (Revelation 3:3). God's Word assures us that this day will not overtake us as a thief (see 1 Thessalonians 5:4).

4. Jesus would not spew His Church out of His mouth, yet He said, *"So then because thou art lukewarm, and neither cold nor hot, I will spue thee out of my mouth"* (Revelation 3:16).
God has called us to be overcomers, to endure to the end, and He has given us the tools to accomplish the task. He has provided forgiveness for us through the cross for the times we fail. He has given us His inspired Word to sustain our faith. He has given us the Holy Spirit to be our helper. He has given us brothers and sisters in our church fellowships who can encourage us. And He is seated at the right hand of God the Father, making intercession for us. In short, God has given us everything that Heaven has to offer to make us worthy to wear the white raiment and to appear before God the Father with Jesus as our Bridegroom.

THE RELATIONSHIP BETWEEN THE IDENTITY AND THE MESSAGE

These things saith he that hath the seven Spirits of God, and the seven stars; I know thy works, that thou hast a name that thou livest, and art dead.   Revelation 3:1

This is the way Jesus identified Himself to the church in Sardis and to the fifth church era. Let us examine the various elements of this identity:

He that hath the seven spirits of God: As I said at the beginning of this chapter, although this church era began so well, the churches of the Reformation quickly fell back into formalism and denominational squabbling, and Jesus declared them to be dead. They maintained a reputation of being alive, but they were dead nevertheless. Their services had degenerated into ritual, formalism and ceremony. This is what happens when churches grow spiritually cold.

Jesus identified Himself in this way because the people of this church needed the seven Spirits of God to bring life to them. It is the Spirit of God that brings life:

It is the Spirit that quickeneth.   John 6:63

The seven Spirits of God are: *"the Spirit of wisdom," "the Spirit of understanding," "the Spirit of knowledge"* (Isaiah 11:2), *"the Spirit of grace"* (Hebrews 10:29), *"the Spirit of life"* (Romans 8:2), *"the Spirit of truth"* (John 14:17) and *"the Spirit of holiness"* (Romans 1:4). The Scriptures also mention *"the Spirit of prophecy"* (Revelation 19:10), but that is the same as *"the Spirit of truth,"* and *"the Spirit of counsel"* (Isaiah 11:2) which is the same as *"the Spirit of understanding."* When any church has the seven Spirits of God operating in their midst, there will be life in that church.

These seven Spirits were in the churches in the days of the apostles, they were available to the Sardis Church era, and they are available to the churches today.

And the seven stars: Jesus still holds the pastors (stars) in His hand. Although many church leaders had wavered, many others had remained true to God. Church history reveals many dedicated servants of God who refused to compromise their faith in Jesus Christ: John Knox, John Oldcastle, William Succling and John Bannister, just to mention a few. These were men who held to the truth and were martyred for their stand.

Some who held to the truth and would not deny their faith were martyred by their own people.

Jesus has had His faithful people throughout every era of church history, and we have the assurance that the gates of Hell will never prevail against the Church.

CHAPTER 7

CHRIST'S LETTER
TO THE CHURCH IN PHILADELPHIA

And to the angel of the church in Philadelphia write; These things saith he that is holy, he that is true, he that hath the key of David, he that openeth, and no man shutteth; and shutteth, and no man openeth.   Revelation 3:7

I find it especially interesting to note the way Jesus identified Himself to this church and this church era because I believe that this church represents the church of the Rapture, the historical era of 1900 A.D. to that great day when we will meet the Lord in the air, and I believe it will happen in my lifetime. In this era, the Church has turned back to the Word of God and has again yielded to the work of the Holy Spirit.

The world in which we find ourselves today is much like it was in the days of Noah, as Jesus said it would be:

And as it was in the days of Noe, so shall it be also in the days of the Son of man. They did eat, they drank, they married wives, they were given in marriage, until the day that Noe entered into the ark, and the flood came, and destroyed them all.
                                                    Luke 17:26-27

Focusing on food, drink and sex seems to be "business as usual" for the people of our world.

Notice that Jesus did not mention family life or children. In former times, people married to raise a family, and then, as fathers and mothers, they dedicated themselves to this task. Today, many couples never even bother to make their union formal with holy matrimony, and many of those who do end up in divorce court. Satan has focused his attack on the family, and the world around us, with its materialistic wealth and instant communications, has given him the tools he needs to do his job well.

Things seem to be going so well in this world that Christians have been rocked to sleep and are neglecting the most important things of life. A great majority of our mothers have left the home in pursuit of a paycheck to help defray the costs of big mortgages, car notes, fancy clothing and the interest to pay for it all. Mothers and children no longer have time to bond with each other. Yes, mothers still love their children, but somehow the accumulation of goods has become the first priority for many. And, if that doesn't destroy the family, drugs will.

Satan has direct contact with our minds and with our way of thinking as never before through the modern communication systems of television and on-line services. A common saying heard in an earlier time was, "The hand that rocks the cradle will control the world." Satan is saying, "Move over, Mother! I will take over here." That concept may sound old fashioned to many, and maybe it is, but it is time to turn back to God and to His Word.

Not all the news is bad. The good news is that thousands of people have turned back to God and He has heard our cry and is pouring out His Spirit upon our churches. People are being saved and filled with the Holy Spirit, and the Gospel is being spread to the ends of the Earth.

We are now in the process of being transformed into the image of Christ so that He may live through us. He has called us out of darkness, and we are no longer the children of the night, nor of darkness. We have discovered the devices of Satan and are watchful for our souls. We have our lamps, and they are filled with oil.

We have done all this because of the hope we feel within our souls, based upon the promise of Christ's soon return:

Beloved, now are we the sons of God, and it doth not yet appear what we shall be: but we know that, when he shall appear, we shall be like him; for we shall see him as he is. And every man that hath this hope in him purifieth himself, even as he is pure.
                                                                1 John 3:2-3

Based upon the prophecies of the Bible, many of us believe that Christ will return by the year 2000 or in the early years of this next century. We will soon know, for the time is here.

THE CITY

Philadelphia was located in a very beautiful valley situated inland about a hundred and twenty-five miles from the coast of the Mediterranean Sea near the Cogamis River. The actual city was built on five hills in this beautiful setting.

Philadelphia did not get its name, as many think, from the Bible. Attalus II, the king of Philadelphia, had a great love for his brother Eumenes, who was the king of Pergamum, and because of this love, Philadelphia was known as "the city of brotherly love."

Philadelphia was one of only two churches for which our Lord had no rebuke. We will see His reasons later.

THE COMMENDATION

I know thy works: behold, I have set before thee an open door, and no man can shut it: for thou hast a little strength, and hast kept my word, and hast not denied my name.   Revelation 3:8

Let us examine the various elements of this commendation:

I know thy works: These words were spoken to every church. Jesus knows our works. He knows everything, small and great, that we do for His glory, and we will always receive more in return than we have given:

And whosoever shall give to drink unto one of these little ones a cup of cold water only in the name of a disciple, verily I say unto you, he shall in no wise lose his reward.   Matthew 10:42

Giving a cold glass of water does not require much on our part, but we can be sure that the reward for doing it in the name of the Lord will be much more than a glass of water. God is the greatest Giver, and He will never allow us to do more for Him than He does for us in return. When we do something for the Lord, our motive is never reward, but the reward is there nevertheless. He knows our works and He rewards our works.

Many look upon the need for works in the Christian life in a negative way. That should not be. When Jesus Christ saved us, He put a desire in our hearts to work for Him:

For we are his workmanship, created in Christ Jesus unto good works, which God hath before ordained that we should walk in them.   Ephesians 2:10

Jesus has a purpose for every born-again believer. He has a place in His vineyard for each and every one of us. We were created in Christ Jesus *"unto good works."* If you can find your place in Christ and work for Him, you will never be sorry. A life of works for Christ is a blessed and happy life.

Christ's Letter to the Church in Philadelphia

Behold, I have set before thee an open door: This is a very important statement and a very exciting one. The Apostle John saw a door opened in Heaven:

After this I looked, and, behold, a door was opened in heaven: and the first voice which I heard was as it were of a trumpet talking with me; which said, Come up hither.   Revelation 4:1

An open door was also set before the believers of the Philadelphia church, and because they represent this present church era, that open door is set before us as well.

John heard a voice that sounded like a trumpet, and through that trumpet-voice God spoke to him. Paul wrote that a trumpet would also speak to the people of our day:

For the Lord himself shall descend from heaven with a shout, with the voice of the archangel, and with the trump of God: and the dead in Christ shall rise first: Then we which are alive and remain shall be caught up together with them in the clouds, to meet the Lord in the air: and so shall we ever be with the Lord.
1 Thessalonians 4:16-17

The thing that John experienced is to be repeated in the Rapture of the Church. God has set before us *"an open door,"* and that open door will be announced by the trumpet.

If it is true that we are living in the Philadelphia Church era, as many Bible scholars believe, then we will experience the Rapture of the Church. There can hardly be any doubt that the Rapture will indeed occur, but just when it will occur has long been a source of contention among believers. There are several competing theories about when it will happen. The important thing is that He will return for His Church. He is not obligated to do things on my timetable or on anyone else's, for that matter. Our responsibility is to be ready when He chooses to come.

The Pharisees thought they understood perfectly the first coming of their Messiah to the Earth, yet when He came, they didn't recognize Him or accept Him. Let us not follow their footsteps. Let us say, "Even so, come, Lord Jesus," and leave the timing of it to Him.

There are many other scriptural teachings that show us the necessity of being ready for that great day:

And when these things begin to come to pass, then look up, and lift up your heads; for your redemption draweth nigh.
Luke 21:28

But of the times and the seasons, brethren, ye have no need that I write unto you. For yourselves know perfectly that the day of the Lord so cometh as a thief in the night. For when they shall say, Peace and safety; then sudden destruction cometh upon them, as travail upon a woman with child; and they shall not escape. But ye, brethren, are not in darkness, that that day should overtake you as a thief. 1 Thessalonians 5:1-4

Behold, I shew you a mystery; We shall not all sleep, but we shall all be changed, In a moment, in the twinkling of an eye, at the last trump: for the trumpet shall sound, and the dead shall be raised incorruptible, and we shall be changed.
1 Corinthians 15:51-52

God has also set many signs in the world which point us to His coming. He has placed Israel as a great timepiece, and we can measure the approximate time of His return by the fulfillment of the biblical prophecies concerning Israel. Jesus Himself said:

Now learn a parable of the fig tree; When his branch is yet tender, and putteth forth leaves, ye know that summer is nigh: So likewise ye, when ye shall see all these things, know that it is near, even at the doors. Verily I say unto you, This generation shall not pass, till all these things be fulfilled.
Matthew 24:32-34

The fig tree represents Israel, and that tree put forth its tender branches on May 14, 1948. As we all know, many nations have since then tried to destroy Israel, but they have not succeeded, and they will not succeed.

Whatever the future brings, we can overcome through Christ. He taught:

And fear not them which kill the body, but are not able to kill the soul: but rather fear him which is able to destroy both soul and body in hell.
Matthew 10:28

With Jesus on our side, we have nothing to fear. He was seen even in Daniel's time by King Nebuchadnezzar. He called Him the *"Fourth Man."* He was walking in the midst of the fire with Shadrach, Meshach and Abednego who had been cast into a fiery furnace for their faith (see Daniel 3:8-27). It is good to remember that not one hair on their head was singed. Jesus has promised each of us:

I am with you all the days, — perpetually, uniformly, and on every occasion — to the [very] close and consummation of the age. Amen.
Matthew 28:20, AMP

Paul informed the church at Philippi:

I have strength for all things in Christ Who empowers me — I am ready for anything and equal to anything through Him Who infuses inner strength into me, [that is , I am self-sufficient in Christ's sufficiency]. Philippians 4:13, AMP

Because Jesus was with them, the apostles suffered without fear or complaint.

And when they had called the apostles, and beaten them, they commanded that they should not speak in the name of Jesus, and let them go. And they departed from the presence of the council, rejoicing that they were counted worthy to suffer shame for his name. Acts 5: 40-41

Church history reveals that the early Christians prayed that they would be counted worthy to suffer for their Lord.

We have many things to look forward to and nothing to be concerned about. We are headed for the Great Marriage Supper of the Lamb, and this will just begin our future life with the Lord.

For thou hast a little strength: This word "strength" in the original Greek means "power." This Philadelphia Church era has a little power although it is not the same power that was evident in the time of the apostles. That doesn't mean that the same power is not available to us. It is, but our faith **has not** risen to that level.

I have personally seen the power of God's presence manifested over and over again, but I still don't believe I have seen the miracles of God performed like the apostles saw them. I have seen God heal the sick. Deacon Robert Campbell of Colfax, Louisiana had a cracked skull after an accident on his job, and after our church prayed, he was healed. A lady who was blind in her left eye was healed instantly. I have seen deaf ears opened and fevers instantly broken. My grandson was brought back to life without any brain damage after he drowned and was under water some thirty minutes. I have seen other healing miracles, but I have also seen failures when we prayed, and I personally don't believe that the apostles had as many failures (when they prayed over the sick and afflicted), as we have had. This Church era does have a little strength.

And thy hast kept My Word: In the days when many were denying the inspiration of the Scriptures or accepting some scriptures and denying others, this Church kept God's Word. James taught:

Be ye doers of the word, and not hearers only.   James 1:22

Jesus was pleased with His Church for having kept His Word.

And hath not denied My name: The true Christian, if given the choice — deny Jesus Christ or be martyred — will always choose to be martyred. No threat exists that could make a true believer deny his Lord Jesus Christ.
Justin Martyr wrote (of the church in the Smyrna days) that when the proconsul would ask men and women who had been arrested if they were Christians and they responded that they were, they were given an opportunity to deny and curse Jesus Christ. If they persisted in their faith, they would be led away to their death. Those that face the Great Tribulation will also be given a choice: deny Jesus Christ and take the mark of the beast or be killed.
Today, many religious leaders and churchgoing people deny the virgin birth of Jesus, deny that He came in human form, deny the atonement of His blood, deny His deity, deny His

resurrection from the dead, and deny His coming again. People who take this stand will be among those who are *"falling away,"* and they will make up the apostate church.

THE REBUKE

As I said at the outset of this chapter, this church received no rebuke. This leads me to believe that this must be the church in existence at the time of the Rapture and that it will be *"without spot or wrinkle,"* something that Jesus said would be true of His Bride.

THE EXHORTATION

Behold, I come quickly: hold that fast which thou hast, that no man take thy crown.   Revelation 3:11

Let us examine the various elements of this exhortation:

Behold I come quickly: Jesus never said that He was coming "soon." He said, *"I come quickly."* When He does come, it will be suddenly:

Behold, I shew you a mystery; We shall not all sleep, but we shall all be changed, In a moment, in the twinkling of an eye, at the last trump: for the trumpet shall sound, and the dead shall be raised incorruptible, and we shall be changed.
                              1 Corinthians 15:51-52

I used to wonder: since Jesus is coming *"quickly"* and we *"shall all be changed, in a moment, in the twinkling of an eye,"* how does this relate to the ten virgins? When the cry went out, *Behold, the Bridegroom cometh; go ye out to meet Him,* how did they have time to trim their lamps? I have come to the conclusion that this is what I am doing right now. I cry out to those who read this book as I do to those who hear me teach God's Word in these days: *"Behold, the bridegroom cometh! Go out to meet Him* [Back in the days of the Smyrna Church, *get ready to meet Him].*" I will continue to cry out for people to be ready until the last call goes out.

I wonder, though, will there be such an urgency in our cry, which may be uttered just minutes before He appears, that people will have time to trim their wicks (deal with minor things) but not enough time to get the oil they need? We must keep crying out and trust that our cry will awaken those who are sleeping. It may well be that a new anointing will come upon us in the final moments of time to make a superhuman effort to cry out to those who are not ready.

Hold that fast which thou hath: One thing could be said of this church. They had something to hold to. If you have something from God, I counsel you to hold it tight and not let it slip away. When the storm comes, and it will surely come, those who have nothing in their hearts from God will be swept away by the powerful forces of Satan. I trust that you will make a determination to stand in that day.

That no man take thy crown: Jesus came from Heaven to Earth and suffered at the hands of Satan and the forces of this world, and He did it for His Church. He did it so that we could be heirs of His promises. He did not want His Church to be robbed of its crown. He bought that crown for us with His own blood. If He loved us that much — enough to pay such a high price for us — we should love Him enough to guard it.

THE WARNING

Behold, I will make them of the synagogue of Satan, which say they are Jews, and are not, but do lie; behold, I will make them to come and worship before thy feet, and to know that I have loved thee.   Revelation 3:9

Which say they are Jews, and are not, but do lie: These men were only Jews in the flesh. They did not possess the faith of Abraham. He was justified by faith, as the Scriptures teach:

Even as Abraham believed God, and it was accounted to him for righteousness. Know ye therefore that they which are of faith, the same are the children of Abraham.   Galatians 3:6-7

These false Jews, Jesus said, were *"the synagogue of Satan."* They thought they could be saved by keeping the Law of Moses. The truth is that the Law of Moses was impossible for man to keep. Only Jesus kept them perfectly. He lived the Law, fulfilled the Law and paid the debt we owed for having broken it. Therefore, He is the only way to eternal life, and those who refuse Him cannot be truly children of faith in God. They may say they are Jews, but they're not.

I will make them come and worship before thy feet, and to know that I have loved thee: Jewish people will worship at the feet of Christ's Church and will know that He loves His Church. Jesus was born of a Jewish mother, and all His earthly relatives were Jews. The prophets who foretold His birth, His life, His rejection, His trial, His death, His resurrection and His second coming were all Jews. Despite the fact that the Jewish people as a whole rejected the Savior, they will turn to Him during the Great Tribulation.

What did Jesus mean when He said that Jews would worship at our feet? The only way I can picture it is when we are in Heaven with Jesus before He returns to the Earth again. We know that we will be with Him when He comes riding the white horse John saw in his vision. He saw armies following Jesus as He rode, *"clothed in linen, white and clean."* This white clothing, I am convinced, symbolizes our presence with Christ, for white garments are a symbol of the Bride of Christ. Prior to this, however, Jews will worship *"before [our] feet."* They will surely not be worshiping us. They will be worshiping their Messiah, but the fact that they are worshiping *"before [our] feet"* indicates to me that we will be seated with Christ on His throne.

The best news is that Israel will indeed turn to Christ and receive Him as Lord and Messiah. Paul wrote:

For I would not, brethren, that ye should be ignorant of this mystery, lest ye should be wise in your own conceits; that blindness in part is happened to Israel, until the fullness of the Gentiles be come in. And so all Israel shall be saved: as it is written, There shall come out of Sion the Deliverer, and shall turn away ungodliness from Jacob: For this is my covenant unto them, when I shall take away their sins. As concerning the gospel, they are enemies for your sakes: but as touching the election, they are beloved for the fathers' sakes. Romans 11:25-28

And not as Moses, which put a vail over his face, that the children of Israel could not steadfastly look to the end of that which is abolished: But their minds were blinded: for until this day remaineth the same vail untaken away in the reading of the old testament; which vail is done away in Christ. But even unto this day, when Moses is read, the vail is upon their heart. Neverthe-

less when it shall turn to the Lord, the vail shall be taken away.
2 Corinthians 3:16

There are many other passages, both Old Testament and New, that confirm this glorious truth.

THE PROMISE

Because thou hast kept the word of my patience, I also will keep thee from the hour of temptation, which shall come upon all the world, to try them that dwell upon the earth.
Him that overcometh will I make a pillar in the temple of my God, and he shall go no more out: and I will write upon him the name of my God, and the name of the city of my God, which is new Jerusalem, which cometh down out of heaven from my God: and I will write upon him my new name.
Revelation 3:10 and 12

Let us examine the various elements of this promise:

Thou hast kept the word of my patience: Because this church had kept *"the word of [Christ's] patience,"* they would be rewarded. It pays to live for God. He spoke clearly about those who heard His Word and obeyed it:

Therefore whosoever heareth these sayings of mine, and doeth them, I will liken him unto a wise man, which built his house upon a rock: And the rain descended, and the floods came, and the winds blew, and beat upon that house; and it fell not: for it was founded upon a rock.   Matthew 7:24-25

The Word of God will sustain us. He is our rock. He is our refuge. He is our high tower. He is an ever-present help in the time of trouble. He has promised:

I also will keep thee from the hour of temptation, which shall come upon all the world, to try them that dwell upon the earth: If we are snatched away before the hour of temptation, if we must endure part of the Great Tribulation, or if we have to endure to the end of that Great Tribulation, God will bring us through. He is able to Rapture us out, but He is also able to make our house stand in times of storm. If it is truly built upon the rock, it will stand — whatever comes our way. Jesus can keep us in the midst of the storm, as He kept the three Hebrew children. He can keep us, if and when we are cast into a lions' den. He brought Moses and the Israelites through the Red Sea, and they didn't even get their feet muddy. If it becomes necessary for us to drink the waters of Marah (bitter waters), God will cast a tree in the bitter water, and it will become sweet. If we just stay close to Jesus, He can protect us from anything that we might have to endure.

What is clear in this passage is the fact: *"This temptation shall come upon all the world."* And what will be the purpose of it? *"To try them that dwell upon the earth."* Jesus gives us a better understanding of this in the other chapters of the Revelation of John (see chapters 6 through 19). Jesus has promised *"to keep [His Church] from that hour."* Those who are not born-again believers will have to face that day without Him.

Him that overcometh will I make a pillar in the temple of my God: *"Him that overcometh."* There it is again. Jesus is telling us that to qualify to be *"a pillar in the temple of God"* we must overcome. No one can overcome this sinful world and its satanic forces without the help of the Great Overcomer. His name is Jesus Christ, and we can only overcome through Him:

For whatsoever is born of God overcometh the world: and this is the victory that overcometh the world, even our faith. Who is he

115

that overcometh the world, but he that believeth that Jesus is the Son of God? 1 John 5:4-5

When I was about ten years old, I went to the same school as two brothers in the community. The youngest of the brothers was my age, and the two of us seemed to always be in conflict. After the first encounter, it became obvious that I could "handle him," but the results were not the same when I came up against his older brother, for he was four years older than me.

The good news was that I also had a brother four years older than me, and in that moment he happened to be on the other side of the school building playing ball. I did the only I knew to do in that situation: I ran as fast as I could, crying out to my older brother to help me. There was no hesitation on his part. He came running and quickly took care of the problem.

Later, I discovered that I had a worse problem, and my older brother was not able to "handle" this one for me. I found myself in a spiritual battle against the world and against satanic forces, and sin was quickly destroying my life. It was affecting not only me but everyone who loved me, and I simply could not overcome the problem.

In July of 1952 I realized that I had to have help. I ran to the only One who could help me. This time it was not my earthly brother. It was the Son of God. I cried out, "Oh God, forgive me! Jesus, come into my heart! I need You!" He had already fought my battle long before I was born and had won the victory. When Satan heard me cry out to Jesus, he knew it was time for him to depart.

Since that time, Satan stands nearby awaiting an opportunity to attack me. He knows that his only chance to destroy me is if he can catch me when Jesus is not around. I don't let that happen, for I know that I am no match for Satan. Since Satan knows that he is no match for Jesus, I don't hesitate to call on Him when I need His strength.

If you recognize your need of help, just call out to Jesus now. He is ready to come to your aid. You can conquer through Him:

Nay, in all these things we are more than conquerors through him that loved us.   Romans 8:37

Will I make a pillar in the temple of my God: This is a beautiful promise. Several years ago I did a study on the pillars of the temple and here is some of what I discovered:

1. The pillars were there solely for their beauty

The workmen melted bronze to set upon the top of the pillars. Then they placed nets of checker work, wreaths of chain work for the "chapiters," which were up on top of the pillars. There were seven wreaths for each chapter set in two rows and they were round about upon the one network, to cover the chapiters that were upon the top, with pomegranates and lily works. When I read this, I get a picture of the beauty God has intended for His people. Jesus is telling His Church that she will possess the beauty of God's Temple.

2. The pillars did not support the temple

Because of the beautiful display of melted bronze, nets of checker works and wreaths of chain works on top of the pillars, and because of the pomegranates and lily work, it would be difficult to see that those beautiful pillars did not support the Temple. The weight of the Temple was not upon the pillars. If, you think that the weight of God's Kingdom is upon the Church you are mistaken. We cannot save, heal, deliver or build a Body of believers. Only God, by the works of the Holy Spirit, and the works that Jesus did for us on the cross, can take a people out of the nations for His name. Jesus told his disciples:

I will build my Church.   Matthew 16:18

And when it was done, He did it:

And the Lord added to the church daily such as should be saved.
Acts 2:47

I am glad that God allows us to work in His Kingdom. He just allows His bride to be involved and then He gives her rewards for her faithfulness. The angels in Heaven would be glad to do what we are doing,

Unto whom it was revealed, that not unto themselves, but unto us they did minister the things, which are now reported unto you by them that have preached the gospel unto you with the Holy Ghost sent down from heaven; which things the angels desire to look into.   1 Peter 1:12

God has planted it in our hearts to work for Him, just as love has planted it in a godly wife to do things for her husband and family.

For we are his workmanship, created in Christ Jesus unto good works, which God hath before ordained that we should walk in them.   Ephesians 2:10

God did all this so that we could be full of joy and stay involved.

All this is another of His acts of grace. So, servants of God, please don't get puffed up and think that you are more important to God than any other born-again believer. God has not put the weight of the world or the Kingdom of God on your shoulders. Just serve Him in the beauty of holiness!

He shall go no more out: My wife, Beth, died and went to Heaven and God sent her back. She told me about what she had seen there and what she had heard. She wanted to stay, but it was not her time. She still enjoys reading in the Bible about some of the things she saw. She says, "Just think, the next time I go I will never have to go out."

And I will write upon him the name of my God, and the name of the city of my God, which is new Jerusalem, which cometh down out of heaven from my God: and I will write upon him my new name: When I read this I feel like the lady who had only a few days to live. She contacted her pastor to discuss certain aspects of her final wishes. She told him which hymns she wanted sung at her funeral service and which scriptures she wanted to have read. She also requested to be buried with her favorite Bible. The pastor was preparing to leave when the lady suddenly remembered something else she wanted to say. "Pastor, there's one more thing," she said excitedly.

"What's that?" the pastor asked.

"This is very important," the lady continued. "I want to be buried with a fork in my right hand."

The pastor stood looking at the lady, not knowing quite what to say. Finally, when nothing more was said, he slowly responded, "I'm puzzled by this request. Could you explain?"

"In all my years of attending the fellowship dinners at the church," the lady said, "when the dishes of the main course were being cleared away, someone would invariably say, 'Keep your fork.' When they said that, I knew that my favorite part of the meal was coming. Sometimes it was velvety chocolate cake or deep-dish apple pie, but always something I looked forward to. I want people to know that I am about to have the best part of the meal."

Not long afterward, at that lady's funeral, the people who were walking by the casket noticed the pretty dress she was wearing, her favorite Bible in the casket with her, and something very strange. She was holding a fork in her right hand. Over and over again, the pastor would hear the question "What's with the fork?" and over and over again, he would just smile and say nothing.

Only during his message in the funeral service itself did the pastor finally tell the people of his conversation with this lady shortly before she had gone into the presence of God. He told them what the fork had symbolized to her. "You can stop thinking about the fork now," he told them, but he was sure that they wouldn't stop thinking about it, and he was right. The next time you reach for a fork, I trust that it will remind you, too, that the best is yet to come.

The name of my God, and the name of the city of my God, which is new Jerusalem, which cometh down out of heaven from my God: and I will write upon him my new name: Although I don't know what these new names will be, I do know that it is going to be a wonderful day when Jesus writes the name of God, the name of the new Jerusalem, the city of God, and the new name of Jesus Christ, our Lord, upon us. All I can say is, hold onto your fork, for *THE BEST IS YET TO COME!*

Jesus identified Himself to the church in Philadelphia and to the Philadelphia Church era as:

These things saith he that is holy, he that is true, he that hath the key of David, he that openeth, and no man shutteth; and shutteth, and no man openeth. Revelation 3:7

Let us examine the various elements of this identity:

These things saith he that is holy, he that is true: Jesus proved this when He came from Heaven and lived a sinless, holy and perfect life. He succeeded, where Adam and the whole human race had failed. His life was holy, and every word that He spoke was true. He showed that He was *The Truth* when He fulfilled all three hundred and thirty prophecies given in the Old Testament by the prophets of God. They concerned His birth, where He was to be born, His coming out of Egypt, where He would be raised, His earthly ministry, His trial, death and resurrection and many other aspects of His life.

He that hath the key of David: In order to understand what Jesus was talking about when He mentioned that He had the key of David, it would be necessary to understand the Davidic Covenant that the prophet Nathan delivered, from God, to King David:

And thine house and thy kingdom shall be established for ever before thee: thy throne shall be established for ever.
2 Samuel 7:16

God spoke to Israel through Isaiah, the prophet:

And the key of the house of David will I lay upon his shoulder; so he shall open, and none shall shut; and he shall shut, and none shall open.   Isaiah 22:22

Jesus said that He was *"holy and true."* That is why He never breaks His covenant, and this *"key of David"* was part of His covenant. Before Jesus can fulfill His Davidic covenant with Israel, He must fulfill the prophecy given to the apostles by the Holy Spirit:

Simeon hath declared how God at the first did visit the Gentiles, to take out of them a people for his name. And to this agree the words of the prophets; as it is written, After this I will return, and will build again the tabernacle of David, which is fallen down; and I will build again the ruins thereof, and I will set it up.
                    Acts 15:14-16

Jesus is reminding the Church that He has taken a people from among the nations (the Gentiles) for His name and formed His church, but He will again turn His attention to Israel. Isaiah said, *"And the key of David will I lay upon his [Christ's] shoulders."* When will God do this? Paul tells us:

For I would not, brethren, that ye should be ignorant of this mystery, lest ye should be wise in your own conceits; that blindness in part is happened to Israel, until the fulness of the Gentiles be come in.   Romans 11:25

When God turns His attention back to Israel, the next two verses of Paul's letter will be fulfilled:

And so all Israel shall be saved: as it is written, There shall come out of Sion the Deliverer, and shall turn away ungodliness from Jacob: For this is my covenant unto them, when I shall take away their sins. Romans 11:26-27

Perhaps the reason Jesus reminds this church era that He had *"the key of David"* is so that we Christians love Israel and pray for the conversion of the Jewish people.

Jesus also holds other keys:

And [I] have the keys of hell and of death. Revelation 1:18

Just as He holds *"the key of David"* to loose the children of Israel from the blindness that has afflicted them over the past centuries, He also holds the keys of Hell (Hades or the grave) and death. Jesus will open the graves that hold the bodies of the saints and will cast death aside. The saints will hear the sound of the trumpet and the voice of the archangel and will be changed *"in the twinkling of an eye."* Those who have preceded us in death will be *"raised incorruptible"* in glorified bodies, just like Jesus, and those of us who remain alive will rise to meet Jesus in the air. We will escape the grave and death, and we will be changed and given glorified bodies.

He that openeth, and no man shutteth: This is the same statement that Isaiah made when he gave the prophecy that "the key of the house of David" would be placed upon the shoulders of Jesus.

So he shall open, and none shall shut; and he will shut, and none shall open. Isaiah 22:22

There is a definite connection between these scriptures that deal with *"the key of David," "the keys of hell and death,"* the opening and closing. This promise is for both Israel and the Church. All this will happen in *"the day of the Lord,"* a seven-year span. Israel and the Church will rejoice together.

When the set time of our Lord comes to open the door of heaven no man can stop it. This is the church era that this will take place. Jesus will come for His bride (the Church) and catch her away to be with Him. To the church he will be the bridegroom. We have known him as our Savior, Lord, Elder brother, Intercessor, Advocate, and other ways, but when He opens the door of heaven and calls us up to meet Him in the air (see 1 Thessalonians 4:13-17), we will know Him as our bridegroom. Then when He returns to Earth we will return with Him (see Revelation 19:11-17). We are the ones mentioned in verse 14 clothed in fine linen, white and clean.

At His return to earth, with His bride, He will return as the King of Kings and Lord of Lords to sit upon the throne of David as the King of the Jews:

For unto us a child is born, unto us a son is given: and the government shall be upon his shoulder: and his name shall be called Wonderful, Counsellor, The mighty God, The everlasting Father, The Prince of Peace. Of the increase of his government and peace there shall be no end, upon the throne of David [David's was an earthly throne] *and upon his kingdom, to order it, and to establish it with judgment and with justice from henceforth even for ever. The zeal of the* LORD *of hosts will perform this.*
Isaiah 9:6-7

Then the Scriptures tell us:

Blessed and holy is he that hath part in the first resurrection: on such the second death hath no power, but they shall be priests of God and of Christ, and shall reign with him a thousand years.
Revelation 20:6

We will be *"priests of God."* Why? Because we love to serve our bridegroom. We have done it on Earth before the Rapture, and we will continue to be *"priests of God and of Christ"* during the thousand-year reign. This word translated "reign" means "to rule with." Paul taught:

Do ye not know that the saints shall judge the world?
1 Corinthians 6:2

At the beginning of the thousand-year reign, the day of the Gentiles will be closed, God will restore Israel. Was that what happened on May 14, 1948? No, what happened that day was just like a shadow of what was to come. It was like the cloud that Elijah's servant saw. It was only the size of a man's hand. That, however, was enough for the prophet. He was sure that it meant that the rain was on the way.

What happened to Israel in 1948 was just a type or shadow of the restoration of Israel. The main event is coming. We have been looking at that tiny cloud since 1948, but when Jesus returns with His Bride at the end of the Great Tribulation and the beginning of the thousand-year reign (and after the battle of Armageddon), we will see the rain (the restoration of Israel). We will also see the complete fulfillment of the prophecy of Joel:

And it shall come to pass afterward, that I will pour out my spirit upon all flesh; and your sons and your daughters shall prophesy, your old men shall dream dreams, your young men shall see visions: Joel 2:28

At that time, God will take away spiritual blindness from His people Israel:

Blindness in part is happened to Israel, until the fulness of the Gentiles be come in. Romans 11:25

At the Rapture of the Church the fullness of the Gentiles will be complete, and God will grant the Jewish people a new heart:

And I will give them one heart, and I will put a new spirit within you; and I will take the stony heart out of their flesh, and will give them an heart of flesh: That they may walk in my statutes, and keep mine ordinances, and do them: and they shall be my people, and I will be their God. Ezekiel 11:19-20

For those who would like to do further studies on the restoration of Israel, consider Jeremiah 32:37 and 33:16, Ezekiel 28:26, 34:25, 28 and 38:8. God has given great promises to Israel, and He will fulfill them all:

1. The Jewish people will be gathered from all nations.

2. They will dwell safely in their land.

3. Judah will be saved (Paul verified this when he said *"all Israel shall be saved,"* Romans 11:26).

4. They will be called, *"The Lord our righteousness."*

Some will say that the Jews have already returned from all nations. Actually, a very small percentage of them have returned. When Israel is restored, the people will all return. They have not been able to dwell safely in their land since the days of Solomon, but they will do so. All of Israel has certainly not been saved, as many Jews do not believe in God's existence, and the Lord is not considered by a great majority of the Jewish people to be their "righteousness," but it will happen.

At this present moment, the Jewish people are much as they were in Paul's day:

For they being ignorant of God's righteousness, and going about to establish their own righteousness, have not submitted themselves unto the righteousness of God. For Christ is the end of the law for righteousness to every one that believeth.

Romans 10:3-4

God will use the Great Tribulation period to awaken His people. When they discover that they were deceived, by putting their trust in the antichrist as their Messiah, their eyes will be opened, and Jesus Christ will enlighten them. This will be God's set time to remove the veil from the eyes of Israel. Then Zechariah tells us of their coming conversion:

And I will pour upon the house of David, and upon the inhabitants of Jerusalem, the spirit of grace and of supplications: and they shall look upon me whom they have pierced, and they shall mourn for him, as one mourneth for his only son, and shall be in bitterness for him, as one that is in bitterness for his firstborn.

Zechariah 12:10

Jesus was referring to the Jews when He said:

O Jerusalem, Jerusalem, thou that killest the prophets, and stonest them which are sent unto thee, how often would I have gathered thy children together, even as a hen gathereth her chickens under her wings, and ye would not! Behold, your house is left unto you desolate. For I say unto you, Ye shall not see me henceforth, till ye shall say, Blessed is he that cometh in the name of the Lord.   Matthew 23:37-39

When the antichrist gets through with the Jewish people, this is exactly what they will say, and that will be the day that Jesus opens the door for Israel to be restored. He will deal with the antichrist and fulfill the prophesy which said: *"Jesus of Nazareth, King of the Jews."* This was the sign that the Romans attached to the cross when Jesus was crucified.

If you are neither a Jew nor a born-again Christian, then God classifies you as a Gentile, and *"the day of the Gentiles"* will be *"fulfilled."* This door will soon be shut, and no man will be able to open it again. Be wise and heed God's Word today. This is His *"accepted"* time:

For he saith, I have heard thee in a time accepted, and in the day of salvation have I succoured thee: behold, now is the accepted time; behold, now is the day of salvation.   2 Corinthians 6:2

Today is your day, and tomorrow the door may be closed to you forever. Millions of people have let this door close, and they are now in eternity. If you don't have Jesus in your life, you are like them. Don't risk leaving this life without Jesus. The door is open, so come on in.

The story has been told of a man that was passing through a

cemetery and saw engraved on a tombstone this message: "My friend, as you pass by, as you are now, so once was I. As I am now, soon you will be. So prepare yourself to follow me." It's only too true.

CHAPTER 8

CHRIST'S LETTER
TO THE CHURCH IN LAODICEA

And unto the angel of the church of the Laodiceans write; These things saith the Amen, the faithful and true witness, the beginning of the creation of God;   Revelation 3:14

I find the way Jesus identified Himself to this church to be absolutely amazing. He was, He said, *"the Amen, the faithful and true witness, the beginning of the creation."* Later we will understand why He made this statement.

The Laodicean church coexists with the Philadelphian Church era. The Philadelphian Church era will end at the Rapture of the Church and that will leave the Laodicean church (the apostate church) as the only church left on Earth. This church, along with other occult groups, will make up *"the great whore that sitteth upon many waters"* (Revelation 17:1).

THE CITY

The city of Laodicea was about forty miles east and inland from Ephesus on the Lycus River. It was located at what is known as the "Gate of Phrygian." Camel caravans came through Laodicea from the East and went down to Ephesus, to Miletus, and up to what is called Izmir, the Smyrna in the New Testament times.

According to Dr. J. Vernon McGee, near Laodicea, going up toward the Phrygian mountains, was the great Anatolian Temple of the Phrygian god, Men Karou. This temple was a center of society, trade and religion. Strangers came from everywhere to trade there.

From the very odd-colored soil that came from the hills around Laodicea, the people took clay and mixed it with spikenard and made an eye salve. This salve was shipped all over the Roman Empire. When scientists tested this soil, their analysis revealed that there was nothing in the soil that gave it any healing value.

The city of Laodicea was founded by Antiochus II (262-246 B.C.) who was considered by the Greeks to be a god, and it was named for Laodice, his wife.

There were a whole series of rulers who went by the name of Antiochus. The Jewish historian Josephus wrote about one such man (who incidentally lived about the time that John received his Revelation) who had all the characteristics ascribed to the antichrist. This man was a Syrian, and He polluted the Temple in Jerusalem by sacrificing swine on the altar. He also set himself up in the Temple to be worshipped as god. This could very well be the same Antiochus who founded Laodicea.

THE COMMENDATION

Jesus offered no commendation to this church.

THE REBUKE

I know thy works, that thou art neither cold nor hot: I would thou wert cold or hot.

Christ's Letter to the Church in Laodicea

Because thou sayest, I am rich, and increased with goods, and have need of nothing; and knowest not that thou art wretched, and miserable, and poor, and blind, and naked.

Revelation 3:15 and 17

Let us examine the various elements of this rebuke:

I know thy works: This was not a compliment, as it had been to other churches. Jesus did not say a single good thing about this church. If the works of the Laodiceans had been good He would certainly not have overlooked them. This is proof that their works were only evil. Let it be a warning to all of us: just as God knows every good work we do for Him, He also knows every evil work we do, and He hates evil.

Thou art neither cold nor hot: What a miserable condition to be in! These people were half in and half out, not standing and not sitting. Try getting in that position and see how it feels. No wonder the Lord told them later that they were miserable! When anyone feels miserable trying to serve the Lord they can know that it is because they are half in and half out. Serving the Lord fully does not make a person miserable. How does Jesus feel about those who are half in and half out? He answered that next.

I would thou wert cold or hot: He wants us to make a clear choice, to be one way or the other, to be either fully in or out. He doesn't want us straddling the fence. People who are in such a position can only moan and groan in misery. They do more harm to the Kingdom of God than good. They drive pastors crazy and discourage the rest of the members of their families from serving God. They cause everyone else around them to be miserable. And because misery loves company, these people, just like the spies who returned from Palestine with a bad report and discouraged all the Israelites except Joshua and Caleb, will affect many other people in the process. Jesus exhorted them to either be on fire for God or to be *"cold."* What did the Lord mean by *"cold"*? When He said *"hot,"* He was referring to the zeal that causes men and women to testify of Him to everyone, and when He said *"cold,"* He was saying that He preferred that those who had no zeal for His Kingdom keep silence and not attempt to confess His name. Since they have chosen the way of the world, they should not pretend to walk in His paths. Their lukewarm spirit brings a reproach on Christ and His Church.

He is not saying that He wants people like this to go to a different fellowship. They have hurt the cause of Christ and the Church enough already. He wants them to either get in or get out. If they refuse to take a stand, to get in or get out, He may be forced to get them out. He does not accept their worship, their praise, their offerings or their prayers. We don't need the help of these people. Later we will see how the Lord proposes to handle such people.

Because thou sayest, I am rich, and increased with goods, and have need of nothing; and knowest not that thou art wretched, and miserable, and poor, and blind, and naked: That's about as plain a language as we could ask for. Our Lord doesn't mince words. He draws a graphic picture of the lukewarm church. He wants men and women to see themselves as they really are. This is important, for when people become lukewarm they somehow can't see themselves in the same light that Jesus sees them.

Because thou sayest, I am rich, and increased with goods, and have need of nothing: These people are sure that they are *"rich and increased with goods."* While this may be a true characterization in the natural sense of riches, to think that they *"have need of nothing"* is appalling. They were badly mistaken. They were rich in what doesn't count for much and desperately in need of everything that really matters in life. How sad that most cannot see this in time!

We are spirit beings because we were made in the image of God:

God is a Spirit. John 4:24

The well-being of our spirit being is always our greatest area of need. Man was not made to live apart from God. That is why Jesus said:

Man shall not live by bread alone, but by every word that proceedeth out of the mouth of God. Matthew 4:4

Just as our earthly body needs to be fed to satisfy and to sustain us in this life, our spirit needs to be fed the Word of God to satisfy and sustain our spiritual life. Man is not fulfilled apart from God, and that was the message of Jesus to this apostate church.

This church had the same problem most people have when they are prospered economically. We become proud, arrogant and boastful. God hates pride:

These six things doth the LORD hate: yea, seven are an abomination unto him: A PROUD LOOK ... . Proverbs 6:16-17

When we feel that we are "rich" and "have need of nothing" that is pride. The Bible speaks of another man who had this same attitude:

And I will say to my soul, Soul, thou hast much goods laid up for many years; take thine ease, eat, drink, and be merry. But God said unto him, Thou fool, this night thy soul shall be required of thee: then whose shall those things be, which thou hast provided? So is he that layeth up treasure for himself, and is not rich toward God. Luke 12:19-21

This man would have fared better if he had done what Paul suggested to the believers at Colosse:

Set your affection on things above, not on things on the earth. Colossians 3:2

When Jesus looked upon these people, He saw them in a very different way and knew their deep need. The worse thing about all this was that they didn't know.

And knowest not: It is bad when people don't know, but they think they know, and you can't tell them because they don't have a teachable spirit. God will have to get their attention in some other way. Jesus told the woman at the well in Samaria, "*You worship you know not what.*" He got her attention when He told her all her past, but until He came along, she had never heard the truth. She thought she was doing fine. The people of Laodicea had heard the Gospel, but their ears must have been dull of hearing in a spiritual sense. They were still in spiritual ignorance.

Thou art wretched, and miserable, and poor, and blind, and naked: The truth is brutal, isn't it? *"Wretched!" "Miserable!" "Poor!" "Blind!" "Naked!"* Jesus did not mention anything about how well they were doing financially. Yet, they were *"increased with goods,"* but with all those goods, there was something else. These people were poor. And added to their poverty were the other elements of their ignorance: wretchedness, misery, blindness and nakedness. It is possible to have earthly riches in this world and still be poor in the eyes of God. If we are not *"rich toward God,"* then we may have many other adjectives, and not very nice ones, attached to our lives. The people of Smyrna were just the opposite of the Laodiceans. They had suffered *"tribulation"* and *"poverty,"* yet they were *"rich."* Just as it is possible to prosper financially and still be poor, it is also possible to be poor in this world and yet be rich in Christ. The sad truth about those who respond to the Gospel is that many poor people are spiritually rich, but many rich people are spiritually poor. They allow their prosperity to cause them to become spiritually lukewarm.

My daddy was the richest man I ever knew, but not everyone saw him in that light. He raised four of us boys and our one sister in a small wood frame house in Louisiana. He got his first public job, with the Louisiana State Highways Department, only after he had reached the age of fifty-five. The highest pay scale he received in his lifetime was sixty-five cents an hour. He was never able to afford a car, so he hitchhiked to and from his work every day.

Daddy never had the opportunity to get a formal education, but he was an honest, hard-working man. Although he had very little of this world's goods, he was the happiest and the most thankful person I have ever known. Many times a day I would hear him say to God, "Thank You, Lord, for my job, for my family, for my house, and for all the things that You have given us."

Our neighbors saw my dad as a man stranded in poverty, but I still view him as the richest man I have ever known. May we be as rich as he.

THE EXHORTATION

As many as I love, I rebuke and chasten: be zealous therefore, and repent.   Revelation 3:19

When Jesus said, "*I would thou wert cold or hot*," that was quite a rebuke. He did it because He loved them, and when He rebukes us it is also a sign of His love. Let us examine the various elements of this exhortation:

As many as I love, I rebuke and chasten: If you are rebuked by the Lord, know that He loves you and wants the very best for your life. He feels toward you as we parents feel toward our children. When our children get involved in things they shouldn't be involved in, we are not happy about it and we have to let them know it. That doesn't mean that we stop loving them. It is because we love them that we must tell them the truth and do or say whatever is necessary to help them see the error of their ways. Those who fail to rebuke reveal their lack of love and concern for others. If God rebukes us, we need it, and we should thank Him that He cares enough to tell us about our need.

Be zealous therefore and repent: Zealousness is the opposite of lukewarmness, but how do we get there? Jesus said that we must repent of our lukewarm attitude. We must do whatever is necessary to get on fire for God. It is a decision. None of us would be happy with a spouse that was lukewarm toward us. What a miserable marriage that would be! Jesus longs for our love and is extending grace toward us. He says to every one of us today, *"Repent!"* Repentance is the road back from lukewarmness.

The people of the Laodicean church age were nearing the limits of God's grace. He was giving them one last chance to repent before He vomited them out, and this He will do if they fail to repent before the Rapture.

THE WARNING

I counsel thee to buy of me gold tried in the fire, that thou mayest be rich; and white raiment, that thou mayest be clothed, and that the shame of thy nakedness do not appear; and anoint thine eyes with eyesalve, that thou mayest see.   Revelation 3:18

Jesus warned these people, for there was still time to repent. Let us examine the various elements of this warning:

I counsel of thee to buy gold tried in the fire: There was a lot of falsehood in the Laodicean church era. The people had bought fool's gold. They were being told that they were alright, but this was a mistaken concept. Is it any different today? Millions of people are being swept downstream by the pressures of popular opinion, by television programs that make it acceptable to use four letters words, by the flood of immorality, pornography, violence, and the homosexual lifestyle that bombard us continually. Satan wants us to believe that the Christian lifestyle is not important, that we can accept the alternative lifestyles and still do well.

Jesus was offering these people real gold, gold that had been purified by fire. He was offering Himself. He was put through the fire during His years here on Earth, and He overcame all the pressure that was put upon Him. He came forth from that trial *"as pure gold."* He was offering Himself to the church, for He is *the way, the truth and the life.*

That thou mayest be rich: These people had been enticed by fool's gold, fooled by *the deceitfulness of riches,* led to believe that things made one truly prosperous. If they were *"increased in goods,"* that must mean they were *"in need of nothing."* Paul wrote to Timothy of such deceit:

Perverse disputings of men of corrupt minds, and destitute of the truth, supposing that gain is godliness: from such withdraw thyself. But godliness with contentment is great gain.
1 Timothy 6:5-6

And white raiment, that thou mayest be clothed, and that the shame of thy nakedness do not appear: This *"white raiment"* was the robe of righteousness that Jesus purchased for the Church with His own blood on the cross. It is the only raiment that can hide our nakedness before God. Christ is our righteousness, and we must appear before God clothed in Him or not at all.

And anoint thine eyes with eyesalve, that thou mayest see: Just as everything else these people depended on proved to be false, the eyesalve they made and exported all over the known world also proved to have no value. Jesus offered them a better eyesalve, one that they could depend on. His light brings men and women into true sight.

That was the true Light, which lighteth every man that cometh into the world. John 1:9

Paul wrote:

Ye are all the children of light, and the children of the day: we are not of the night, nor of darkness.   1 Thessalonians 5:5
When we choose to follow God, He causes us to walk in His light.

THE PROMISE

To him that overcometh will I grant to sit with me in my throne, even as I also overcame, and am set down with my Father in his throne.   Revelation 3:21

If the Laodiceans would only repent and become zealous for the Lord, they could overcome. The alternative was to be rejected. The promise to overcomers was made to each of the churches and to each of the church ages. We can overcome in every situation, for our victory is in Christ.

This promise was not made to quitters, to backsliders, to unbelievers, to murderers, to fornicators, to homosexuals, to liars, to the fearful, to the abusers of mankind, to evildoers or to the abominable. It was made to those who overcome all these temptations and live for Christ. How can we possibly overcome all the hate, greed and lust that has infested this world? Only through faith in Jesus Christ. He has already overcome Satan and the world, and He invites us to come to Him, to learn His voice and to follow Him. He will lead us to the Father's house.

He makes a plea to all who will hear Him:

He that hath an ear, let him hear what the Spirit saith unto the churches.   Revelation 3:22

Are you listening to what God is trying to tell you? If so, ask God to enlighten you to the truth of the Gospel through His Spirit. Repent and ask Jesus to come into your heart right now. He will do it, and He will also give you an ear to hear what the Spirit of God is saying to His Church.

THE RELATIONSHIP BETWEEN THE IDENTITY AND THE CHURCH

These things saith the Amen, the faithful and true witness, the beginning of the creation of God;   Revelation 3:14

This is the way Jesus identified Himself to the church of the Laodiceans and to those in the corresponding church age. Let us examine the elements of this identity:

These things saith the Amen: Jesus identifies Himself as the Amen because Amen means truth. The church in Laodicea had been so deceived that the people needed God's truth. Jesus is Truth personified. He said:

I am ... the truth.   John 14:6

He has proven Himself to be true and faithful to His people over and over again throughout history. We can trust Him when we can't trust anyone or anything else.

The faithful and true witness: The Father in Heaven sent Jesus to Earth for the following purposes:

1. To overcome Satan and the forces of evil in the world system

2. To be *"the express image of [the Father's] person"* (Hebrews 1:3)

3. *"To give his life a ransom for many"* (Matthew 20:28)

4. To overcome death and the grave (see Matthew 28:1-9)

5. To sit at the right hand of God as our Mediator (1 Timothy 2:5)

6. To come again the second time as the King of kings and Lord of lords.

Christ was faithful and true in the first four of these responsibilities, and He continues to serve faithfully as our Mediator, and just as surely as He has accomplished these, He will also come again. We can rest assured that He will keep every promise He has made, for He is the Faithful and True Witness.

The beginning of the creation of God: The church in Laodicea, as the apostate church of the Laodicean era, boasted that they were *"increased in goods"* and had *"need of nothing,"* but Jesus was letting them know Who created it all. Without Him, we would have nothing. He made the world we live in, the soil that our food comes from, the air we breathe and the clothes we wear. He created everything:

In the beginning was the Word, and the Word was with God, and the Word was God. The same was in the beginning with God. All things were made by him; and without him was not any thing made that was made. In him was life; and the life was the light of men. John 1:1-4

Too many times, when people prosper and are promoted, they become arrogant and puffed up. Saul had that problem after he became king over Israel. God was not surprised by that.

He often warned the people of Israel to be careful when they prospered:

But Jeshurun [Israel] waxed fat, and kicked: thou art waxen fat, thou art grown thick, thou art covered with fatness; then he forsook God which made him, and lightly esteemed the Rock of his salvation. Deuteronomy 32:15

This description might fit many churches today. It is time for us to preach prosperity with balance and with fear and trembling. It is not wrong to prosper, but it is wrong to forget God when He has prospered us. If we can remember who created it all and honor Him, staying humble and giving Him praise in all things, and if we can give to the poor and support the Gospel, God will gladly continue to heap riches on us. If we are wise, we will not concentrate on the riches. Instead we will pray, "Dear Father God, do what has to be done, but please don't let us miss Heaven."

When Jesus said that He was *"the creation of God,"* He had something else in mind. The insidious teaching of evolution has risen in stature in our time until it is almost universally accepted. This atheistic teaching is taught to our children now in every public school and on popular children's television programs. It is currently Satan's number one weapon against young people, and the apostate church is helping him to use it.

There are two explanations for the origin of the universe: the one, evolution, is sheer speculation that cannot be proven and the other one, the Creation, is a divine revelation from God. I have no problem accepting the revelation given in God's Word. He was the One doing the creating, so He should know how it was done.

Many Christians have embraced the theory of evolution and

this proves that they will be part of the apostate church. Nobody can believe that God's Word is true and believe in evolution at the same time. One day every person who has ever lived on God's planet Earth will know that His Word was true and that evolution is a lie, but for now, we must accept it by faith.

Sixty years ago scientists began to send radio signals out from the Earth into space hoping that aliens from some other planet or universe would hear it and send a message back, proving that there is intelligent life elsewhere in our universe. I believe that at a "set time," there will indeed be a message received, and it will say: *"This is the I Am, the beginning of the creation of God."*

THE ADDED ELEMENT

So then because thou art lukewarm, and neither cold nor hot, I will spue thee out of my mouth.   Revelation 3:16

In many ways, as we have seen, the letter to the Laodiceans parallels the other six letters. There is, however, an added element in this letter which is absent in the others. It is a note of judgment. God will spew this church out of His mouth.

The Greek word translated here as "spue" is *emew*. It literally means "vomit." This church made Jesus sick to His stomach. To spew them out of His mouth meant that He rejected them.

Paul, talking about the condition of the church at the return of the Lord, wrote:

Let no man deceive you by any means: for that day shall not come, except there come a falling away first.
                                          2 Thessalonians 2:3

Those who are caught up in this great falling away will make up the apostate church. Who are they?

1. They are those who were in the church but have departed from the faith.

Now the Spirit speaketh expressly, that in the latter times some shall depart from the faith, giving heed to seducing spirits, and doctrines of devils. 1 Timothy 4:1
This know also, that in the last days perilous times shall come. For men shall be lovers of their own selves, covetous, boasters, proud, blasphemers, disobedient to parents, unthankful, unholy, Without natural affection, trucebreakers, false accusers, incontinent, fierce, despisers of those that are good, Traitors, heady, highminded, lovers of pleasures more than lovers of God; Having a form of godliness, but denying the power thereof: from such turn away. 2 Timothy 3:1-5

2. They are those who were in the church but were unbelievers.

Knowing this first, that there shall come in the last days scoffers, walking after their own lusts, And saying, Where is the promise of his coming? for since the fathers fell asleep, all things continue as they were from the beginning of the creation.
2 Peter 3:3-4

3. They are those who were in the church but were never born-again.

For the time will come when they will not endure sound doctrine; but after their own lusts shall they heap to themselves teachers, having itching ears; And they shall turn away their ears from the truth, and shall be turned unto fables.

2 Timothy 4:3-4

These are scoffers or mockers. They deny the inspiration of the Word of God, the virgin birth, the atonement in the blood of Jesus, His bodily resurrection and His Second Coming. What a dangerous position to take! No wonder God declares that He will reject them.

CHAPTER 9

WHAT THESE LETTERS MEAN TO US TODAY

When I received an unction from God to write this book, I knew that I was not an experienced book writer, and I would have had no reason to write this were it not for God's grace and glory. As I prayed about why He wanted me to write it, I sensed that it was because I would not be influenced by anything except the truth of His Word.

I can't say how many will profit spiritually from this book, but I have profited by it immensely myself already. Seeking God for exactly what He wanted to say — through prayer and study, with many tears and also with times of laughing — has caused me to spend more time alone with God than I spent in the previous forty-seven years of my ministry. My life has been changed as a result. For one thing, the Holy Spirit has cast a spotlight on every flaw in my character, and I have become determined to give God His rightful place in my life from now until He returns for His Church.

A few years ago, while I was asking my heavenly Father to help me understand every word as I studied the Bible, He said to me, "Studying the Bible is like taking a trip. The faster you travel, the less you are able to see." Since that time, I have begun to live by every word that I read and I have enjoyed it immensely.

As I travel, I take time to look around me, to see what is transpiring, to see what I am missing. Often I have stopped to ask the

Holy Spirit, "What does this mean?" and He has taken me to some other scripture that enlightened me.

Although many things were said in these short letters to the churches, a few things stand out. The principal seems to be that we must overcome in this present world if we expect to be part of God's family in the next. Satan tries to make us think that is impossible, but it's not. Jesus came into this world to make us overcomers, and with Him by our side, we will be victorious.

With His vast riches *"in glory,"* Jesus equips us with everything we need to live above the strife and sin of this present age, and as we fellowship with Him continually, we grow in knowledge and understanding. What motivates us is the knowledge that we will live with Him forever. Our destination is the New Heaven and the New Earth, and making the journey there with Jesus, feasting on His Word, is a joy that words cannot describe.

In ourselves we could not achieve this, but Christ has made provision for us to be transformed into new creatures, to become *"a new creation"*:

> *Therefore if any person is (ingrafted) in Christ, the Messiah, he is (a new creature altogether,) a new creation; the old (previous moral and spiritual condition) has passed away. Behold, the fresh and new has come!*   2 Corinthians 5:17, AMP

Now is the time of salvation for you. If you have not been saved, confess Christ now. Say these simple words from the heart:

I believe that Jesus Christ is the Son of God.
I believe that God has raised Him from the dead.

Now, pray with me this simple prayer:

What These Letters Mean to Us Today

Father,

Forgive me for my sins.
Jesus, I invite You into my heart. Please come in and save me
now.   *Amen!*

If you prayed this prayer from your heart, Jesus is now your Savior. He said:

That if thou shalt confess with thy mouth the Lord Jesus, and shalt believe in thine heart that God hath raised him from the dead, thou shalt be saved. For with the heart man believeth unto righteousness; and with the mouth confession is made unto sal-
vation.   Romans 10:9-10

You have not been justified by any good thing you have done, but by your faith in Jesus Christ, the only Begotten Son of God:

Even as Abraham believed God, and it was accounted to him for righteousness. Know ye therefore that they which are of faith, the same are the children of Abraham.   Galatians 3:6-7

Overcoming Satan in this world is not difficult as long as we are traveling with Jesus. It is only when we begin to think that we can reach our destination without Him or we decide to take control of the journey that we find ourselves in trouble. He is the Shepherd, and we must let Him lead. He knows where every pit is located, and although He seems to choose rough roads for us to travel, we have nothing to fear when He is by our side. Trust Him:

Trust in the LORD with all thine heart; and lean not unto thine own understanding. In all thy ways acknowledge him, and he shall direct thy paths.   Proverbs 3:5-6

Just as He knows all the pits along our way, He also knows where every treasure is located, and He knows just when to let us find one of His precious jewels. He has at least one for each and every day. In His great wisdom, He does not allow us to find them all in one day. He always holds some in reserve, and this makes our trip more exciting and enjoyable. We look forward to each day.

What a joy it is to walk with Jesus every day. And when each day is finished, we always have the next to look forward to. We can be assured that we will never wake up and find Him gone. As long as He is with us we can enjoy all things and endure all things. And, when we have, at last, come to the end of our earthly journey, it is not the end, but the beginning. There will be so much more awaiting us in the next life.

Be assured that as you make this journey through life with Jesus Christ our Lord, it will be exciting, loving, peaceful, joyful and victorious. You will only make this journey once, so ENJOY IT WITH JESUS!